The Good Life in Galicia 2017

Cyberworld Publishing

www.cyberworldpublishing.com

E-book ISBN: 978-0-9953961-3-5
Print ISBN: 978-0-9953961-4-2

~

Cyberworld Publishing
Panton, Lugo
Spain

The Good Life in Galicia 2017

An Anthology

Edited by S. Bush

CONTENTS

Cover Image   7

Introduction   9

Non Fiction   11

In the Market by Fiona Cowan   13
     (First place non fiction)

You Can Teach an Old Dog a Trick or Two
     by Andrea Jones   27
     (Second place non fiction)

Eight Days Wandering on the Camino de Invierno
     2017 by Bronwyn Cole   44
     (Third place non fiction)

The Stray Dog AKA Bruno by J. P. Vincent   59

Fiction   65

The "Santa Compaña" by Noelia Roca Jones   67
     (First place fiction)

Guerillas Come in Many Different Shapes
     by Robin Hillard   71
     (Second place fiction)

What Colour is your Tractor by Gary Gaunt   79
     (Third place fiction)

Wild Horses by Olivia Stowe   83

Poetry

101

The Rampant Calabaza by Liza Grantham   103
(First place poetry)

The Elements for the Heaven
by Adrián Casanova   104
(Equal Second place poetry)

Our Peaceful Village by Liza Grantham   105
(Equal Second place poetry)

My Dog Chased a Fox by Liza Grantham   107
(Third place poetry)

A Drop by J. P. Vincent   108

Molten Tempest by J. P. Vincent   110

The Barn by Liza Grantham   111

Girl Talk by Liza Grantham   113

About the Authors   115

The good Life in Galicia 2016   119

Cover Image

The Good Life in Galicia 2017 cover image is taken from this photo by David Magdalena. It shows the famous apartment building on Toralla Island in Vigo and was taken at sunset from Samil beach in January 2017.

Many thanks to David for the use of this photo.

Introduction

Now in its second year this anthology, *The Good Life in Galicia 2017*, and the competition behind it, began in 2016 as an idea for a competition to encourage people to write about Galicia and raise awareness internationally of this fascinating part of Green Spain. As we are an English-language publisher, the stories had to be in English, and to make it easy, entrants did not have to have lived in Galicia or to have even visited here. These requirements remained the same for the 2017 year, but we added a poetry category, as Galicia, one of the Celtic lands, is a land of poets.

We were pleased in 2017 to have had entries from as far afield as Australia and New Zealand as well as entries in all categories from Galicians.

There were outstanding contest entries in each category and our judge, Olivia Stowe, had a difficult time choosing her winners. Winner in the fiction category was Noelia Roca Jones, with The "Santa Compaña", in the non fiction category, the story "In the Market", by Orkney Islander Fiona Cowan, was the winner. In poetry the winner was Liza Grantham's amusing poem about vegetables, "The Rampant Calabaza".

The bulk of this anthology comprises competition entries with the addition of works written especially for this anthology by Olivia Stowe and J.P. Vincent.

We hope you enjoy this second brief look at an ancient land, one full of generous people and natural splendours, and agree that there is indeed a lot of good in a life in Galicia.

~

NON-FICTION

In the Market

by Fiona Cowan

Each day in Lugo Province, Galicia, there was a market. Somewhere. Mondays in Trabada, Tuesdays in

Vilalba, Wednesdays in Ribadeo, Thursdays in Muimenta, Fridays in Burela, Saturdays you could nip over the Ría to Vegadeo and on Sundays return to Meira, or Barrieros. The towns filled with vans, tractors, lorries, and even handcarts as farmers' wives brought their fruit and vegetables (including huge bunches of grelos, turnip tops, eaten nowhere else!) and their lovely free-range eggs. The cheeses were easily followed by their smell and the meats followed by the flies. A whole pig's face, vacuum packed in a flattened form and hung up on a stall to grimace down on those who passed by. Vegetarian pilgrims on the Camino de Santiago averted their eyes as they trudged through the markets, carrying backpacks adorned with the shell of St James.

In the same markets there were stalls for every other possible purchase, every size of underwear or socks ("Three pairs for two euros, Guapa!") every tool or ornament, and shoes from stilettos to the wooden suecos, the clogs still worn by Galician farmers.

Sandra loved the market. She often travelled further afield on her day off just to see a new market, although the Moroccan clothes stalls seemed to be the same in each major market. Sometimes all the marketeers were in Viveiro on the first week of the month for a mega market. She loved it!

Her students in the academy where she taught were so curious to know what she bought when she was home in the UK, which markets she went to, but the truth was she hardly ever shopped in markets at home. Apart from Camden Town and Portobello Market, the only ones she knew of were the farmers' market the week before Christmas and the German Beer Fest with its wooden cabins. Like all of her friends, she did her weekly shop in Tescos. That was why she so enjoyed Galicia and the fantastic foodstuffs she gathered each market day. The best part of her new job, teaching English in Galicia, was that she only began work in the afternoon, so mornings were for shopping, mostly in the nearest market.

One of her students, Guillermo, was a quiet but studious type. He smiled as he listened to her teach and always ventured to reply to the questions she posed to his group. He struggled with the phrasal verbs—all 4,000 that appeared on the web page she recommended—but then so did every student of English. His favourite part of class was the idiom of the day. He wrote them all down with glee. Another archaic word he seemed to like.

When she first began teaching at the academy, she was glad to have adult students. There were no rules to prevent her socialising after class. Week by week she got to know students over tapas in one of the local bars. For the students it was like a free class, so they usually paid for the drinks. For her it was a chance to hear more about Galicia, and the culture in their different peublos. Guillermo wasn't able to stay very late. She knew he had a daughter and he had to return home before bedtime. There was no mention of a mother but she didn't like to pry.

One afternoon the lesson centred on "There is . . ." and "There are . . ." A bit tricky when the Spanish only had one phrase replacing them both. "Hay . . ." could be used to say how much there was of anything singular, plural or uncountable things like salt, milk, or sea. She found herself asking how many people there was in each student's house. "There are two in my house," responded Guillermo. Interesting, she thought, knowing his daughter lived with him.

Weeks passed. She settled into Galicia and she began to see it as her home. In the processions of Carnaval she was greeted by students who waved to her from their Charanga bands as they passed, blowing on their kazoos. She was greeted by the parents and grandparents of her students. Although they spoke no English, they wanted to thank her for helping their family members. Everyone needed English for work, to get a job or a better job. She felt she was helping. She knew she had gained more respect here in Galicia than she had at home in the UK. But some days she felt a bit isolated, almost lonely. She noticed in the market that everyone else was shopping in pairs, sisters, friends, mothers with daughters discussing the lomo or the chorizo, choosing together. She wondered if she would ever have a friend in the market.

Putting her thoughts towards that afternoon's B2 class, she tried to use phrases with locations: I'm all at sea, I am at a crossroads, I am over the moon, I am in the market for. . . . The list went on. Not all had Spanish equivalents, so she explained them one by one. Each classmate had to write down an example based on their life or experience. Rosa was finished first and keen to share. "I am over the moon because I have tickets to visit Scotland this year!"

One of the other students muttered something that sounded like Ryanair didn't fly that high. Sandra ignored the remark and praised the effort. Another student, Pepe, was at a crossroads in his life, trying to look after his elderly father and keep his job. At that point the class reverted to Gallego, while advice was given on chicas, whom he could employ to help with his father or residencias where his father could be taken to live. Sandra realised she had lost the moment and gave up. Although she could follow basic Spanish, once the local Galician language erupted, there was no going back. Sandra noticed Guillermo speaking to Pepe after the class broke up. She realised Guillermo had not answered any of the questions. As he left the class she called out that they should bring their answers next week as homework.

The following Tuesday she received their homework to mark. She saved Guillermo's until last. He had answered well and honestly, not that it was necessary. Fiction was acceptable. The only phrase she queried was when he had written, "I am not in the market yet." She didn't mark it as incorrect but she put two question marks next to it. ¿? It didn't really make sense. Then they were back to routine English in preparation for the next exams, due in a month.

A very pretty face greeted her as she stepped out into the Saturday crowd that weekend. "Good morning, Señorita, how are you?" After realising she was being greeted in English rather than Spanish she smiled at the teenager and replied in English—wondering how far to go before the speaker would get that confused look. She

17

needn't have worried. The girl had a very good level of English: a slightly American accent but a huge vocabulary. She had obviously been told Sandra was a teacher and, like many of the youngsters, was hoping for extra classes, preferably free.

"I have come to introduce you to my grandparents," she announced. "They have the best vegetables in the market, and today they also have honey." Sandra saw no harm in following her. It was broad daylight and nothing was going to happen. She turned to her young companion and asked her name. "I am Rocio," came the reply, followed by a joke, "like the dew, I am best in the mornings." Sandra marvelled at her easy nature, chatting away in English and passing remarks on all the stalls they passed. Sandra felt relaxed to have a friend alongside to discuss the produce. She found herself asking what some of the cheeses were called, and the girl not only knew the names but also offered helpful comparisons. "More or less like Brie, but stronger. A bit like Feta but drier," explained her companion.

Before they reached the grandparents' cart Sandra thought about asking her what she wanted, how had she picked her up from outside her flat, and how she knew she was an English teacher. But it seemed so direct and so un-British, so she decided to wait. In the next aisle she was rewarded.

"Abuela, te presento la Señorita Sandra Stevenson, profesora de mi papá." The wrinkled dame beamed a huge smile and began thanking her for the help she gave to her son. Unsure which son she was referring to, Sandra kissed both the wizened cheeks proffered and studied a face that bore no resemblance to any of her students. All will be revealed, she thought and the next moment saw the grandfather approaching, the very face of Guillermo, only slightly more weathered but just as gorgeous. In forty years time if Guillermo looked like that she would still fancy him, she thought. The old man had a winning smile and his eyes, as blue as Hemingway´s old man of the sea's, twinkled at her. He didn't wait to be presented. He grabbed her hand and then offered the traditional dos besos. Or probably the 'dous bicos' as they were known in Galicia.

"¡Encantado conocerte, Sandra!" he announced, letting on that he had already heard her name. So, Guillermo might be the quiet type but he obviously spoke to his father about his teacher. She felt suddenly included in this wee family. They were obviously the grandparents on the paternal side, and she knew nothing of the other grandparents or Rocio's mother.

The grandparents were already busy selling their new season's honey, so Rocio gestured they should continue their circuit of the market. Rocio explained that her granny didn't want any help with the job of selling, as she had high hopes for Rocio and wanted her to keep up her English. "Where did you learn such good English?" Sandra asked, relieved at least to know who this girl was.

"Mostly from school, I suppose, but my mother used English in her work and then sent me to spend several summers with people she knew in the UK through her work. My accent, I am sorry to say, comes from the little Mermaid and other Disney films. Papá suggested I come shopping with you to learn a bit more of your accent. He really likes it."

Sandra wondered again how to ask about the shadowy mother figure, but was unable to phrase a question without asking what her mother used to work at, or where she went to, or where she now was. Still, she felt her heart lift at the idea that Guillermo liked her accent and had obviously spoken well of her to his daughter and his parents. She decided to return the following week and buy some honey, hoping his parents would recognise her.

She suggested to Rocio that they have something in the café across the plaza and sit down a minute so she could assimilate all this new information. Rocio was more than happy to be invited, and they found a table where they could sit under the sunshade but leave their ankles in full view of the sun to brown them up for summer. When the waiter took their order, he enquired if Sandra was Rocio's aunt. The teenager replied that of course not, she was an English friend, and again Rocio felt touched that this girl she had just met was already claiming her as a friend.

Sandra resisted asking Rocio what her father was doing that weekend, but she did ask if he was worried abut his exams. Rocio said he was studying hard as he wanted to do well, she added that she helped him a lot and insisted they speak English at home after his classes. That might explain why his homework was often more accurate than work he wrote in class. How funny to have role reversal, where the kids checked the homework of the parents. Rocio told her he had been promised promotion if he achieved the level B2 in his next exam. This would be a huge help to him, not only as he would earn more, said Rocio, but also that he would not have to pay the academy fees for his English classes.

This came as a shock to Sandra. She had assumed all of her students would continue studying with her all year. She had hoped most of them would return next year for their C1 exams even if they passed B2 next month. The fees, she knew, were expensive even though she handled no money, Laura in the office took care of all that, but several of the younger adults were being paid for by their families in the hope of work either here in Galicia, but more likely in Sheffield, or some other UK location. She wondered if she should run optional extra classes using different British accents. However, today the thought that Guillermo might do well and leave the academy filled her with mixed emotions. She would love to see him pass, as he worked so hard, but teaching his class without him would feel like someone had switched off the lights. She must get a grip, she decided.

After the coffee, they resumed their circuit of the market Sandra felt emboldened to try on a jacket she had noticed. There was no mirror on that stall, but today she had a female supporter to give an opinion. The jacket was gorgeous, but, as she feared, it was a bit small. It said large, but she reckoned that was large by Indonesian standards, judging from the label of origin. The stall holder told her he would bring XL next week, "Sin problema."Meanwhile, the two stall holders either side of the jacket stall were watching the performance of the blonde struggling to get her arms out of the sleeves.

"¡Más zapato, menos plato!" called the man on the right, indicating she should buy a pair of his trainers. Rocio made a swift retort after explaining to Sandra that 'more shoe, less plate' was the local advice on how to lose weight. The guy on the left held out a plate of his delicious chorizo and encouraged her to ignore this advice, his hand gestures told her she could afford to put on a bit of weight as far as he was concerned. Back at home she would have taken offence and got on to her high horse about treatment of women in public. But here? She actually didn't have it in her to fight, even if she did have the language. She accepted a piece of chorizo and smiled at the greasy butcher. (Or whatever job title you gave to men who made these embutidos.)

In the following weeks the students had to prepare for their four exam activities, writing, reading, listening, and speaking. She was now adhering to the fixed lesson plans, and the students had to talk and write about topical issues rather than more personal experiences or opinions. She knew the exams required students to hold certain views on such diverse topics as education, culture, child rearing, and renewable energy. This year the list included suggestions of refugees and civic duties. Students were advised not to express strong political opinions in their monologue or dialogue exams, as one never knew who the examiner would be and it was silly to fail an expensive exam just to score a political point. All very un-British Sandra felt as she corrected the practice papers where each student recited the same careful opinions and 'sat on the fence'. She mentally added that phrase to her list for next year's class on locations, but what had Guillermo meant when he said he wasn't 'in the market yet'?

Rocio was often in the market. She hadn't called at Sandra's door again, but as soon as Sandra approached the grandparents' stall, she would see Rocio waiting and they would spend time looking around together. The bigger jacket did indeed arrive, but to her shame, Sandra needed an XXL. She decided it was between a size 12 and a 14, so what size would her curvy mother need?

Finally, the exams were over and her class presented her with a bunch of flowers from the market. She recognised these by the newspaper that the flower man used to keep the stems wet in the heat. There were promises of eggs, onions, and potatoes from the family huertos if the students passed. There were careful expressions of optimism on how the exams had gone, but nobody could possibly know. They opted to have a week off while recovering and awaiting the results. Sandra felt really flat that week. There was not usually a high pass rate, as the students were not all at the same level, but she was worried that this, her most advanced class, should do well and show to the academy that she was a good teacher. Pepe told her he was definitely leaving that term, as his father had been accepted into a care home and it would be very expensive. However at least he could keep his job, and he thanked Sandra for her help.

"In fact," he said, "without your class I would never have found the care home, so thank you for that also." Sandra was now totally lost and asked what on earth he was talking about now. "Don't you remember?" he said. "Guille told me all about the residencia and how fantastic it was to caring for people with Alzheimer's." So that was the conversation they had had in Gallego at the end of class, She lost so much in conversations where her basic Spanish could not follow the slide into the local language. What experience did Guillermo have of Alzheimer's disease? Both his parents seemed coping really well from what she could see.

At that moment she decided to cross the cultural bridge and ask Pepe what he meant. The man was leaving her class and she might never see him again. He could only tell her to mind her own business. "What experience does Guille have of that Residencia?" She enquired, holding her breath a little.

"Sorry, we thought you knew. His wife developed dementia at thirty-eight, a very clever woman and a great mother. but sadly there is no treatment and it was impossible for him to care for her."

"Was?" asked Sandra. "I mean, what happened to her? Is she still there or in a hospital?" It was beginning to make sense, the way Rocio spoke of her mum in the past tense, just memories.

"She died two years ago, sadly. Guille has been alone and working hard to pay off the debts of her care. He was able to tell me there was a vacancy last month when he went there to pay off his final payment. There is usually a waiting list, but because of Guille being in my class, I had enchufe with the owners, and my father got the room." There it was, 'enchufe,' the connections in Spain that spoke louder than words.

When the results were posted on the academy notice board, the teaching staff were first to read them. It had been a good year, all twelve of her B2 level had passed, mostly with 8 out of 10 or 'notable,' as the Spanish deem such an achievement. But three of her class had been awarded 'sobresaliente,' with 9 points. In fact, in two of his exams Guillermo had scored a 10—listening and speaking.

If he had taken Rocio to help with his written papers, he would probably have been a straight 10 in all four, with a score of 100 percent. She felt so proud of him, no doubt her favourite student, but with a sad heart she realised he would be leaving her class and, probably, her life.

The academy owners were delighted with her and already signing up new students for her class based on her success. She returned to the classroom after all the congratulations were over and the students were gone, and she saw a pile of things on her desk. Sure enough there were sufficient vegetables, plants, and fruit gifted to her to open a small stall herself. She noticed a jar of honey from Rocio's grandparents' stall. It had been left sitting on a jotter at the corner of the desk. She wondered why he had left his homework book for marking if he wasn't coming back. She opened it carefully and her heart skipped a beat as she read what he had written:

'Now again I am in the market—please will you have dinner with me tonight in Casa Miguel?'

You Can Teach an Old Dog a Trick or Two!

By Andrea Jones Jones

August, 2010

"Have you seen the posters?" my friend Barbara asked. I was on my coffee break when she popped into the estate agency where I worked.

"I don't think so", I replied. "What's it about?"

"John and Mike are organizing a car boot fair in Goián next month", she told me.

This was exciting news indeed. I had heard of these legendary events that had sprung up in the UK in my absence. I had left the UK at the tender age of seven and had lived here in Galicia since I was eight. For many years I had no idea of all the exciting things I had been missing, as I had no contact with other British people. I had never had

English television and could count on the fingers of one hand the trips I had made to visit family over the years.

When I started working in the estate agency I came into contact with people from all over the UK, as well as from other countries. Apart from having made some wonderful friends, I had the opportunity to speak English and hear firsthand news of life in the UK. In some respects, it was bewildering and these strange creatures were like aliens——like when they rang to make an appointment to view houses and asked me if it was OK if they arrived at 2:00 p.m. I mean, don't these people know I lock up the office at 2:00 and drive home for a two-hour lunch break with my family? Don't they eat? Don't they have families? What kind of country keeps its offices open continuously from 9:00 till 5:00? What kind of country closes its offices at 5:00? At this time I was only into my first hour of a four-hour afternoon shift. .. . Hmmmm, now that is something to think about. Anyway, I am getting sidetracked here.

The morning of the event I appeared at the venue with a group of Spanish friends. It was a little more sparse than I had imagined. (In my fantasy I had seen a nice green field, with hundreds of cars neatly arranged into rows, which was a bit unrealistic as I knew the square in Goián was roughly tarmacked and had space for ten cars at a pinch.) My friends straggled along, bemused, as I rushed about buying English books (in English, I might add), comics for my children, and a couple of ornaments because I got carried away. I normally am not a fan of ornaments and they duly found their way back to my own version of the car boot fair when it got going.

I really enjoyed it and was delighted to discover there was going to be a repetition of the event, partly due to the popularity of the first event, but mostly because so many people had only heard about it after it had taken place! This is a very common occurrence here in Galicia. In fact, I always refer to my most-hated section in the local paper, but one I compulsively read, as "What you missed out on last weekend!"

I asked for and duly obtained permission from the organisers to have a small stall of my own. I excitedly told all my friends and students about the coming event. My enthusiasm must have been catching, as a couple of friends and students asked if they could join me. I checked that this would be OK with John and Mike, and they seemed quite positive about the idea. However, word of mouth here works miracles, and a couple of days before the event I became uncomfortably aware that my "couple of friends who were joining me" now threatened to outnumber the original members. I tried to shrug off my misgivings and tell myself the more the merrier, although deep down I wasn't sure everyone would share this philosophy.

I nagged and nagged everyone who was coming with me to be on time, as Spanish punctuality differs greatly from the British version, and on the morning they had all arrived on time, except one of my dearest friends. I managed to dot them about amongst the other stalls so the Spanish contingent didn't look so obvious. I sort of hid Jorge and Marta behind their camper van, convincing them that was sure to be the most popular spot, which they just accepted as crazy British logic as they did extremely well.

I had just started to feel more relaxed when an unfamiliar car weaved its way among the stalls, getting well-deserved dirty looks from all the other stall holders who were busy putting the finishing touches to their displays. I felt myself cringing as I recognised my missing friend, Paqui, and tried to hide behind my stall. This was quite difficult as my grand stall consisted of a small single leaf camping table and a little wooden card table. As Paqui spotted me, she stuck her head out of the passenger side window, yelling, "Yoo hoo, Andrea, here we are. Look, I've bought Ángeles with me, too".

I put a brave face on, made a space available next to me, and got them sorted with as little further disruption as possible. I had only met Ángeles a couple of times before, as we didn't really move in the same circles, but we had close friends in common and we got on really well. It was a great day, enjoyed by everyone, I think. And I realised that it was about so much more than making a euro or two. It was a social occasion for many friends and acquaintances to meet, the little bar did a roaring trade, some of the people were really excited about their finds on the stalls, and the stall holders had a great sense of success, even though the actual takings were meagre as the prices were so low.

And that was that, or so I thought. A thoroughly enjoyable experience that I was lucky enough to share with my friends and students. How little did I know then, what would become of all this.

* * * *

A couple of weeks later I had a phone call from an unfamiliar number. "Sí?" I answered. "It's Ángeles", a vaguely familiar voice replied. I rapidly racked my brain trying to remember if it was one of my students, but after a couple of seconds I was none the wiser, so I timidly said "Dime" (which is the familiar way of inviting someone to confide in you, hoping to gather more information and thus work out who exactly Ángeles was!) I guess my ignorance was apparent as she immediately cleared up the mystery for me. "You know, Rouco's partner (still no idea), Senda's friend. She gave me your number (by now I am getting really worried as she may be running out of clues). We were at the English market in Ferreira together?" Finally, the penny dropped!

Before I had a chance to say anything, she launched into this rapid explanation of why she was calling. "I had a meeting with Severino (the mayor of Monforte) and told him what a fantastic idea this was. I'm trying to convince him to let us do one in Monforte. He is quite enthusiastic about the idea, but I'm not exactly getting across what I'm on about. Anyway, he said, "Bring one of the English people involved with the market in Ferreira to see me and explain precisely what it is you want to do." So, as you are the only English person I know, I thought perhaps you would come with me and explain the whole concept."

As she paused slightly to take breath, I tried to explain I wasn't exactly "involved" with the Ferreira Car Boot Fair,. I just happened to know the people who were and got permission to do a stall. She ignored this timid intervention of mine and carried on as if I had agreed. "We have to meet him tomorrow evening at 7:00 p.m. at the town hall. You can tell him all about the philosophy behind the venture so he can see what a good thing this will be for Monforte if we can hold one monthly."

By now I'm really panicking. I'm sure I'm not good at getting a point across, I'm nervous of personal meetings with people in "Authority", and most of all, I just thought it was fun thing to do on a Sunday morning. I'm not sure there is a "philosophy behind the venture".

I protest feebly, because if there is one thing I dislike more than having personal meetings with people in "Authority", it's letting people down. I try again to explain that I don't really know much about the issue and that I don't think I'm the right person for the job. "But it has to be a 'real English' person, and you're the only one I know, and anyway, the others don't speak Spanish", she wailed.

I felt myself weakening. I'm a real sucker for lending a hand. "OK. But I'm still not sure I will be much help."

"That's marvellous. Thank you so much. I'll meet you tomorrow at 6:50 p.m. outside the town hall door. This is going to go ahead", she cries enthusiastically. By the time I finish the phone call, I'm feeling dizzy and a bit sick. 'Isn't it time you learnt to say NO, kindly but firmly?' I say angrily to myself.

"I'm meeting the mayor tomorrow", I bravely tell my children. They all look at me in horror as if it's like going to see the headmaster at school but a lot worse because the mayor actually has the power to fine you or even have the local police arrest you. "Why? What have you done?" my eldest son says.

"I haven't done anything!" I exclaim, incensed that he should even think his law-abiding mother could have done anything wrong. "I'm going with Ángeles to explain what car boot fairs are and why we should hold one every month in Monforte."

"Well, what are they and why should we?" says one of his sisters. Good question. I need to think about this! "Well . . . it's all about one man's rubbish being another man's treasure." (I'm sure I have heard this somewhere before and it certainly fits in with my joyful experience of obtaining eight books I hadn't read, in English, for 4€.) At this point the children lose interest, although I'm sure I see the two boys exchanging a grin that seems to say, 'Mother has got herself into another sticky situation.'

After a sleepless night worrying about things like, "Why do I do these things?", "What actually IS the philosophy behind the Car Boot Fair?", "Did she mean the front door or the side door?" and a long day of showing houses in obscure locations, I find myself standing by the town hall, at a strategic point where I can see both the front and side doors, punctually at 6:50 p.m. The minutes pass— seven o'clock, five past. I start to wonder, "Should I ring Ángeles?" "Will I recognise her?" "Is there another door I don't know about?" "Can you be fined for keeping the mayor waiting?" when thankfully I see her walking towards the main door.

She greets me warmly, giving me a hug and a kiss and thanking me for coming. We go up to the mayor's office, where he also greets us both warmly, giving us a hug and a kiss and saying to me, "Oh, I know you! You're a friend of Senda's. We have all been out together at "El Couto" (a nice little bar that used to be by the swimming pools where they had live music on Friday nights) and I used to see you a lot at "Los Molinos", which is my friend Senda's house. It's a fascinating place, built in the eighteenth century and used as a tax office. The house itself is full of spyholes and musket holes, which were installed to guard the precious documents and the taxes deposited there, beautiful furniture, curiosities, and paintings. It's open to the public and parts of the old stables have been converted into a lovely rural bed and breakfast.

We all sat down in comfortable chairs round the table and he looked at me expectantly and said, "Right, explain to me exactly what it is you want to do." I didn't feel that it was appropriate to say that actually I didn't want to do anything. I was quite happy working at the estate agency and teaching. But as I had given the matter some (well, a lot of, actually) thought, I realised that, rather than a car boot fair, what appealed to me more was a flea market, where alongside secondhand stalls, there could be craft stalls with handmade items and fresh, locally grown fruit and vegetables.

This seemingly odd combination of things was largely due to the people I know and mix with. Most of my friends, like myself, believe in recycling, ecology, and sustainable economy. We like to eat fresh seasonal local produce, and although I live in a flat and no longer grow my own food, I lived on a small holding growing up and my family and I were pretty self-sufficient. Many of my friends do grow their own fruit and veg and I'm lucky to be given plenty of their surplus produce. I also know a lot of people who live alternative lifestyles, who are hippies or bohemian, who are fantastic artists, musicians, and craftspeople, but who find it difficult to sell their wares.

There were no secondhand shops here then, no charity shops, nowhere you could sell or donate unwanted items. Spain had been in economic recession since 2008 and showed little sign of improving, and I thought a flea market would be good for so many people struggling to make ends meet. So, this basically is what I talked about. The mayor was very receptive. Many of the things I talked about appealed to him. Ángeles was enthralled with my ideas as she herself is an amazing artist. She has a very hippy dress sense and her long-term partner, Carlos Rouco, was at that time the president of the nonlucrative organization Salvador Allende, a charity that worked closely with poor communities in South and Central America. Sadly, this hardworking and committed man has passed away since then.

A month later I got another call from Ángeles, saying we had to go together with the mayor to a meeting the following evening at 8:00 p.m. in the premises of the CCU. The CCU was an association of shopkeepers (the initials stand for Urban Shopping Centre in Spanish) who had a relevant role in local politics and were very protective of little local shops. They strongly try to promote shopping locally, and although they have had some great initiatives towards this end, I didn't always agree with some of their methods, which I considered bordered on coercion.

At this stage, I was still under the impression that I had just helped Ángeles out in trying to get the concept across and that it was all nothing to do with me. I tried telling Ángeles this, but she was having none of it. She said Severino had stressed the importance of this being more of a cultural event than a commercial event; that it was about building bridges with different groups of people, many of whom find integration difficult and that it was a totally British concept.

Me and my big mouth! All these things (except for the British bit, as I had no idea if many, or indeed any, of the Brits that had come to live in this part of the world shared my views on these topics!) had been the very words I had used in my sales pitch to the mayor when I was defending Ángeles' proposal for a market in Monforte.

We scurried along after the mayor, finding it quite difficult to keep up, as he's a tall man who walks in long purposeful strides and both Ángeles and I tend to be on short side, while he insisted on the importance of getting the CCU on our side. He knocked briefly on the door and walked into a room with seven serious-looking people who looked up at us unsmilingly. He briefly introduced us, said we were there to present our idea for a flea market in Monforte, made his excuses, and left. I felt he had thrown us to the sharks, and if I hadn't felt so intimidated I would have left, too. But I sat down as they politely invited us to do and waited for Ángeles to explain. She did. She said, "Andrea represents a group of English people who would like to share a little of their culture with us. Tell them about it, Andrea."

I had no idea who the people I was supposed to be representing were, if indeed they considered flea markets to be part of their cultural heritage and much less if any of them had any interest in sharing this odd venture with the local Galician population.

I had great reservations about what the local population would actually think of the idea, as Monforte has always been a somewhat conservative place and at the time anything second hand (other than cars and dwellings) was rather looked down on. I recalled one of my sisters-in-law, embarrassed and apologetic, saying she hoped I wouldn't be offended if she offered me some baby things from her children when my first child was born. Offended!

36

I was delighted and I loved the fact that my child was using things that had belonged to his little cousins. But again, I digress.

So, I rambled on and on about my thoughts about sustainable economy, about how too many useful items ended up in the rubbish because there was no way of passing them on, how people who were hard up could make a penny. I'd even had an idea about the funding for the school trips, which, as a single parent, I found difficult. I thought the children could do a stall where they sold things their family had donated, to my mind a much better idea then selling unwanted T-shirts and lighters to family and friends. Anyway, the meeting was a huge success. One of the main men was the president of the PTA (although to be honest, in Spain there are no teachers involved unless they are also parents!) at his kids' school and loved my idea for raising funds. We not only got their full support, but they also promised to promote our event on their website and newsletter and offered us the use of the council huts, acquired for themed markets, which they were in charge of. Their support at the time was of vital importance.

* * * *

A couple of weeks later, I got yet another excited phone call from Ángeles. "The council have approved it, we just need the secretary to write up the public announcement, display it, and then they will let us know when we can hold the first one! Let everyone know!" I was very happy at the good news, but the last sentence confused me. Who was I supposed to be contacting? How was I supposed to contact them? And, most of all, why should I be doing this? I was now beginning to wonder at the wisdom of getting involved with Ángeles and I also understood the worried looks I had seen passing between my friends, Paqui and Senda, when I first told them of my involvement in Ángeles's project and their unusual lack of enthusiasm. I relayed my questions to Ángeles in quite a shirty manner as, by now, I felt she was taking liberties. Her reply was, "I haven't been able to find anyone to take part. I have told lots of people, but they aren't interested, they don't approve and they don't want to be involved."

I completely understood their feelings. And I realised they all obviously knew Ángeles a lot better than I did when I got inveigled into this crazy scheme. Surely, the first step of the process would have been to find a group of people who wanted to take part before taking the matter up with the mayor, wouldn't it? But it was too late now for me to back out. Somewhere along the tortuous way I had somehow acquired a sense of commitment to the project. "I'll see what I can do," I said somewhat grumpily.

I spent the next week or so getting in touch with a wide variety of people and was amazed at how many incredible people I had got to know over the last few years. I had found a couple of people who were willing to do secondhand stalls, including Jorge and Marta, who I had treated in such an ungenerous manner at the Goián event. I resolved to make sure they got the best spot this time round to compensate. I had a lovely German friend, Emmely, who made the most delicious homemade fruit jams and juices; another German couple, Barbara and Martin, who had a magnificent plant nursery; Frank and his son, Lee, who did the most amazing woodwork. There were also a few Spanish people who had contacted me after being informed of the project by the mayor, who ran a cultural association called "O Colado do Vento". Besides organising numerous cultural events, they also ran a communal vegetable garden, which used only traditional and organic methods in Sober. Two of the people selling their surplus produce were from Cataluña and from Madrid and one was Galician. It made for a really interesting group which was our biggest achievement. I didn't want us just to be a little group of English people.

* * * *

February 2011

After several long weeks of hearing no news from the town, while reassuring the people who had been kind enough to commit to coming that the event would take place, I received a phone call from Ángeles on Wednesday, the 9th of February. "We can do the market this Sunday."

Great, I thought, but it would have been nice to have a little more time to prepare for the event, as it seemed a bit last minute to inform everyone. Before I had a chance to comment, she continued, "By the way, I'm not in Monforte. I'm doing a course in Burela. So, you'll have to go on Friday evening to the CCU premises to get the keys for the huts. Let me know how everything goes!"

At this stage I didn't know whether to laugh or to cry. I contacted everyone, apologizing for the short notice but stressing how important I thought it was that as many of us as possible attended because we had been working so hard for so long to get the venture going. Everyone was wonderful. Now all I had to do was worry about collecting the keys. I duly collected them and placed them safely in the glove compartment of my car so I couldn't inadvertently forget them on Sunday morning.

Then I discovered there was still plenty more to worry about: "Would I be able to open the huts?" "Would everyone turn up on the right day at the right time?"; "Would the local police fine us for driving up and down the pedestrian area, which was the only access to the huts for loading and unloading?" "Would we have sufficient space to manoeuver our vehicles?"

Many of these concerns were due to the fact that the huts in question were an investment made by the town council, supposedly in the style of those used for the famous German Christmas markets, and they had been placed in the small main square. This was not the best location. The square was small and only had access by driving up and down the pedestrian streets. Not a good idea with heavily loaded vehicles. Besides which, they were rather unattractive and, as there were nine in total, they pretty much filled up the square.

None of the residents and local shopkeepers were happy with the initiative. Another thing was that they had arrived in November, in time to arrange a couple of very poorly attended themed markets, but during the summer the square was in constant use for show and concerts, which was now impossible. On the morning of the market, we discovered the biggest drawback of all: They were extremely difficult to open, as the whole system, which consisted of a very heavy top flap that had to be raised and then propped up by the two doors, which folded back, with great difficulty to support it. It took a minimum of three people to open each hut, and one needed to be very tall and very strong. Fortunately, our motley crew did include a few tall, strong gentlemen, who kindly helped the rest of us inadequate beings out.

I woke up at 7:00 a.m. on Sunday morning to torrential rain that never let up all day! But, in spite of this bumpy start, our market was a success. It has taken a long time to convince the local population that second hand is cool. Largely, this has been achieved by some of the outstanding people we have had as members. Some wealthy, some moderately famous, many with very successful professional careers. We have had so many wonderful times over the years: musical events, workshops, raffles, games, storytelling, picnics, and so much more.

Nowadays, things are very different, as there have also been many conflicts, obstacles from the local council, and other problems. But the Sunday market is still going strong. It has really changed Sunday mornings in Monforte, which were dead (with even few bars opening until early afternoon), for the better. We have been featured in numerous newspaper articles, and we became a reference for many other towns that started their own markets, some with greater and some with less success than others. I am very proud to have been a part of all this, even if unwilling at first. And most of about 80 percent of the secondhand stall holders today and about 75 percent of the clients are local Galician people, so it just proves that, with patience, you can teach an old dog a trick or two.

Eight Days Wandering on the Camino de Invierno 2017

By Bronwyn Cole

In September 2015 I walked the whole of the Camino Frances from St Jean Pied de Port to Santiago de Compostela. The experience changed my life and the Galician part of the journey was my favourite. In 2016 I returned to Spain, and to Galicia, for a Workaway placement and first heard about the Camino de Invierno. In July 2017, once more in Galicia, my partner and I spent eight days walking a section of the Invierno route from Monforte to Santiago. Here's a bit of an account of that journey.

July 2nd:

John and Jax drop us off in Monforte, where we take time to look at the Sunday rastro before we start walking. They've kindly let us leave a lot of excess weight at their house—this time I'm not being silly and I'm travelling light. 2015 taught me a lot!

It's a bit late by the time we finally get going—after 10:30 a.m.—and it's already hot, but we are buoyed by the excitement of being on the Camino again. The first shiny new mojon we encounter tells us it's 121 kilometres to Santiago. In the guidebook, the day's stage from Monforte is a thirty-one-kilometre walk to Chantada, where there are more services available. It was never our intention to go that far—we know we aren't very fit and I have an old foot injury slowing me down.

Half of that distance is our aim, and we know we'll have to find our own 'accommodation'. After leaving the city we find ourselves walking totally through rural areas, only encountering small pueblos and aldeas. Taking it leisurely, we stop for a siesta in a large, shady portico attached to a church building. It's elevated and we can see Monforte in the distance.

At 4:30 p.m., having climbed higher and found a very welcome fountain of fresh, cool water, we can still see Monforte in the distance. By 6:00 p.m. it's day over—I've calculated our position to be about fifteen kilometres from Monforte, and we've found a very disused-looking bus stop on the outskirts of yet another aldea. It has a roof, it has a bench seat, and it has a concrete floor. In the circumstances, it will do—who knows how much further we might have to go to find anything else? It becomes our dining room and our bedroom and, with the sun still streaming hotly through the Plexiglas back wall, we settle our tired bodies into our sleeping bags.

For a quiet country road there is a surprising amount of traffic in and out of the aldea, but no one stops to ask us what we're doing . . . or to offer any hospitality.

I thought I would be so tired I would sleep through anything, but when the sun finally goes down, the thoughtfully positioned street light across the road takes over, shining in brightly. Then every farm dog from every aldea within earshot (and there are many) finds a reason to bark furiously and repeatedly, and repeatedly. Finally, I find that the purpose-bought light summer sleeping bag I am in is wholly insufficient for the chilly and misty early morning hours, and, likewise, the yoga mat on the seat is no substitute for a mattress. I give up on sleep and while away the darkness watching insects in the street light.

July 3rd:

As soon as there's enough light to see, we're up, packed, and off. There's thick mist everywhere, which reduces the views but makes walking a lot cooler. Today we're covering the rest of the distance to Chantada, which involves a very steep descent of several kilometres to cross the river Miño and an equally steep ascent on the other side to reach our goal. What draws us on, despite the lack of sleep, is the promise of a coffee at a riverside bar in Belesar that has been recommended to us.

Never have ten kilometres seemed so long, with the descent down to the river through forest and then the bodegas everything we were expecting in terms of difficulty and then some. But, finally, Belesar comes gloriously into view. Now to head straight to that bar! Only to find that it's closed on a Monday for staff to rest and today is . . . MONDAY. This is melt-down territory for my partner, who runs on coffee. Not only is the bar closed, but the mist, that had kept things cool all the way to the river has also now instantaneously lifted, it's hot, and there's the prospect of a two-and-a-half kilometre uphill slog in front of us. There's NO WAY my partner wants to do that, and he's not shy about telling me!

We cross the bridge, and I am (reluctantly) mentally preparing myself for what's ahead, but Fernando has other ideas and he accosts the first vehicle to come across after us. It's a nice young fellow who works amongst the bodegas, and he's very happy to take us to the top of the hill on our quest for a coffee—apparently there's another bar there which may be open. It ends up not and we have to walk a few kilometres further on, all the way to Chantada, for that precious coffee. But the van ride saved us from hours of effort and toil when our energy levels were already low, and as this is primarily a be-kind-to-the-body journey—unlike 2015—I don't feel too bad about 'cheating'.

Tonight there is a real bed, a private bathroom, and the proprietress of Hostal Yoel has even offered to put washing through for us free of charge—is this heaven or what?!

July 4th:

What a difference a good night's sleep makes!

The Camino is all uphill as it takes us away from the town and back into the country and off-road, but it's by no means rigorous with our energy restored. Again, we are breaking up a one-day stage in the guidebook into two, and today's destination is the hermitage at the top of the 1,181-metre mountain of O Faro. Again, we are expecting to sleep out.

It's a pleasant country walk, though the temperature is climbing, to reach the pueblo of Penasillas, where there is a communal fountain complete with hand-laundry pool, which I realise is still being used for the purpose, as it is quite cloudy with soap powder! In fact, the lady who has been doing her washing there and whom Fernando approaches with his perennial question, turns out to be the owner/operator of the local bar and agrees to open up so we can get a coffee. It really does help to be travelling with a native Spanish speaker!

The climb to O Faro begins in earnest after Penasillas. It ascends on a dirt road through woodland above the village, which then emerges to join the tar-sealed road to the top, which is even steeper! We stop at this junction in the shade of a big tree to rest and refuel a little. Then it's on and up and, in the end, walking between patches of shade where we rest a little each time. Fernando talks about getting a ride again but there aren't any cars. Towards the top it starts to get confusing—there is an avenue of large crosses heading straight up the hill on our left, which looks significant, but, in the absence of signage, we ignore it and keep walking up the road.

A little further up and to our right, amongst the trees, is the sound of running water. It's another Godsend fountain of fresh, cool, and drinkable water on this scorching day. Shoes off, feet in, water splashed everywhere! Bliss! Restored, we take to the road again, but a little further on it forks and a Camino mojon indicates we should take the right side, which is heading back down and which, when followed, takes us to picnic tables on the other side of the fountain.

There's absolutely no signage for the hermitage. Alright, we're tired and hot: let's lunch break and then reassess our options. When in doubt, read the instructions . . . the guidebook does mention the crosses, and it seems silly to have got this far and not gone to the top (one option!) So off we go again—up the hill and between the crosses in a straight line . . .that went on and on, this time taking ME close to meltdown territory with its physical demands in the hottest part of the day.

Suddenly we're actually there, on the flat top, with the hermitage in the middle and, to Fernando's delight, an open refugio facing it. Accommodation sorted!

July 5th:

We wake to a clear day at the top of O Faro, but we are looking down onto a blanket of white in all directions. Setting off, it's not long before we're dropping into very thick mist again, which is obliterating all of the wonderful views possible from this elevation. The many windmills along the ridges are scarcely visible, even though we are virtually walking under them, and quite spooky.

It's uneventful walking, slowly dropping down the forestry roads and then through more farmland, and around midday we walk into the prosperous-looking agricultural pueblo of Rodeiro, nestled amongst the hills.

My yoga mat didn't get any softer on this second night out, though the refugio was a vast improvement on the bus stop, and I'm looking forward to another bed! Though at one point, when I was awake in the early hours, I looked out towards the hermitage and absolutely directly above the cross on the apex of its roof was Venus, shining bright and mysterious.

July 6th:

Today we're going to be ambitious and attempt the full guidebook stage of Rodeiro to Lalín because it's only twenty-one kilometres—a routine daily distance for us on the Camino Frances—but one we've yet to do this time.

Out of Rodeiro we're quickly back in the country, which is that lovely Galician mix of woodlands and fields and stone walls. The Way takes us onto an old Roman road under a canopy of trees and, stopping here for an outdoors breakfast, we encounter something completely unexpected and thus a little shocking at first—it's another pilgrim (!), who has deviated from the Camino Frances onto the Winter Route, where they join in Ponferrada, as he does not like all the things associated with the large number of people travelling the Frances. He chats for a few moments and then walks on and we never see him again.

Looking through a gap in the trees, we can see a mountain in the distance and just make out a row of windmills along the ridge—it's gratifying to realise that only twenty-four hours ago we were walking up there! Later in the morning, as we pass through another aldea, Fernando stops at an open barn door to ask the farm worker why the cows are all inside and not out grazing in the sun (where we think they should be). "Wolves" is the answer. The worker wants to know what we're doing and seems a bit nonplussed at the answer. "Wouldn't you rather be working with cows? It's a good life."

The day goes on, all country back roads and trails. We pass a mountain that's being extensively carved up into building stones. Large pig sheds make their appearance with increasing frequency—when we finally reach the centre of Lalín, there is a life-size bronze street sculpture in homage to this very important part of the local economy.

But reaching Lalín was not without a little drama. We must have walked fifteen kilometres—we're on a stretch of unsealed back road that has a lot of up and down to it. It's hot, there is very limited shade to be had, and a certain person's need for coffee is growing. A solitary vehicle approaches heading in the opposite direction, and of course is flagged down; a conversation is had, and the driver offers us a lift. Fernando then makes two very basic mistakes:

1.   ASKING me if I WANTED a ride, and
2.   Assuming I had understood, perfectly in my limited Spanish, what had transpired in the previous conversation.

WHAT I THOUGHT was being offered was a lift to another nearby aldea, where there was an open bar, for an infusion of caffeine.

I had read the guidebook. It clearly stated there were no services of this sort to be had between Rodeiro and Lalín. Coupled with the man's appearance, I find it impossible to trust that the offer is bona fide. Plus, aren't we supposed to be WALKING this Camino? Under pressure to decide, I ANSWER the QUESTION with a NO.

Oh dear, not the right answer AT ALL!

With a shrug (the mystery of women), the potential ride disappears down the road and I have no trouble understanding that what has just occurred is the reason "I prefer to walk the Camino by myself".

We trek on—hot, dusty and cross with each other. I puzzle over what has transpired and finally realise that the ride was being offered to LALIN—probably a five- or ten-minute drive away but on foot, and on this trail, much more; much, much more! When I check out my newly acquired understanding I am met with disbelief—"Of course, what else?!"

It begins to cloud over and a cool wind picks up. The relief from the heat is tempered by the realisation that there is a large thunderstorm brewing behind us and heading our way.

Could I be any more popular?

I pick up my pace, and thinking that maybe I can outwalk a drenching brings a fresh burst of energy to my tired legs. More than two hours later we reach the pavements leading into Lalín.

What absolute relief! All the more so, as all we have received from the accompanying thunderstorm has been a light sprinkling of refreshing rain as it veers away to our left and disappears.

A beautiful twelfth-century church comes into view and I feel uplifted and renewed.

July 7th:

The stress of yesterday has melted away with COFFEE, food, a shower, a good night's sleep, and our first Mass on this route in the centre of town last evening, in the only church that we've found open so far.

Today, the goal is Silleda, about sixteen kilometres away. The Camino leaves town through a network of walking/cycling tracks following the river. Many people are out exercising along it in the early morning. Lots of locals are one thing but then, suddenly, we start to encounter other pilgrims! And not just one or two but heaps! How strange! Up until now we have been walking in a 'bubble', feeling that we are the only ones making this journey and really enjoying the space and the quiet we have been gifted. The change is so abrupt it's a bit hard to take! But the speed at which we walk guarantees that we will be quickly and quietly left behind.

For a while, the route runs closer to main highways—there's more traffic, more industrial activity, more buildings in general. Now we are seeing road signs for Santiago. That's exciting!

There's also a sense of the end looming and a return to 'ordinary'.

But not just yet!

Back in complete countryside again, we are led through an area of reserve on the side of a very deep gorge with the sound of a substantial river running through the bottom. A feat of engineering, in the form of a railway bridge spanning the gorge, comes into view, but what I find really special is the small and unassuming Roman bridge crossing the river a little further along, complete with original stone paths for some distance before and after it. Coming from New Zealand, I find anything this old and still in use is quite awe-inspiring and warranting a surfeit of photos from all angles!

Leaving the Taboada reserve, we come upon an aldea with an OPEN BAR. While we're putting it to good use, several other groups of pilgrims arrive. Then, close by, there's a Romanesque church, also open and dispensing credencial stamps. Other pilgrims visit with us. I can't quite decide if I prefer sharing the increase in services or having 'nothing' to ourselves.

In Silleda, we're staying in our first real true albergue (with albergue prices), but it's luxury in that there's only three beds in our room and we end up with just us in it.

Yes, there are other pilgrims now (get over it!) but this is NOTHING like the Camino Frances!

There's a fiesta in town tonight, and the dancing display from the local dance school becomes my second highlight of the day. Afterwards, we head to a bar to fill up on good local food and then wander back to the albergue, contented in the growing dusk. It's balmy out and much better in the room with the window open for air. That's about when the thunderingly loud disco music part of the fiesta begins—without end for the rest of the night.

July 8th:

The only good part about being kept awake for a significant portion of the night is the early-opening bar in the street this morning, catering to those who have purposely gone without sleep. For the first time, we can commence walking AFTER a coffee and, today, how welcome is that?!

Ponte Ulla looks about right to aim for, though in the guide's altitude profile we see that there is going to be another river crossing reminiscent of the Miño once we get there.

Already Fernando is calculating how to get a ride up out of the valley, but this is our penultimate day and I'm determined we are going to walk to Santiago. Besides, when I do the maths to support my argument, it's clear this is likely to be a much lesser task. Plus, we're battle-hardened now—surely?

The morning takes us through fields of maize, to the doors of another Romanesque church, which is closed (surprise!) and back into woodland. We begin the descent down to Ponte Ulla, and, yes, it's steep and a bit gruelling on the knees. A good way down a side road goes off to our right, leading to another hermitage with a picnic area, running water, and, Lo!, another open refugio all set in amongst trees with the sound of the river below. Right now it's looking like the only place two hot and tired pilgrims should be. Even if only for some food and a wee siesta.

I'm lying there thinking about it—I know there's beds down in Ponte Ulla. The guidebook says so. How much further down I don't know, but I suspect not much, though every distance not covered today adds to the next. On the other hand, it's so lovely and peaceful amongst these trees with their dappled light in the soft breeze.

It really is our last chance to sleep surrounded by nature unless we don't reach Santiago tomorrow and that's unlikely. And it won't cost anything!

The scales are tipping.

The day begins and ends on a first as I now freely CHOOSE to spend tonight under the shelter of the refugio. Later, as the gas cannons heralding the fiesta in THIS pueblo echo and roar up the gorge, I know the choice is the right one!

July 9th:

In the morning, Ponte Ulla is a quick descent on fresh legs.

Behold the morning-after-the-fiesta bar that is open on an otherwise sleepy and silent Sunday! The back entrance to a bakery is open, big containers of large, round, and very fresh loaves stacked ready for the delivery van to collect and disperse. We buy a smaller, more refined type of loaf to take with us (weight still counts!) though, to me, the big ones look more appealing.

The climb up from the pueblo isn't that difficult at all and soon we're in Outeiro, where there's another restorative fountain. The Way winds on between field and forest. A solitary mountain appears—Pico Sacro—which our guide suggests we might like to detour and climb. Not today, Señora!

We're Santiago-bound and it was still at least twenty-one kilometres away when we left this morning. For us, that's a long day! It's after 10:00 a.m. when we come upon a sign advertising a restaurant/bar in the pueblo of Lestedo. We're ready for a break by now but there's a problem—to get there requires us to walk 600 metres out of our way (and therefore another 600 back).

A 'discussion' ensues: one member of the group is advocating going for certainty, the other conservation of energy and trusting in Providence to come up with the goods ON the Camino. In the end, the need to rest and refuel NOW wins out and we walk the required 600 metres—turns out a good decision—the food is delicious, cheap, and plentiful (a little too much so!); coffee excellent;

and I'm sure the basket bearing big chunks of fresh and tasty bread is from the large loaves we saw in Ponte Ulla! What perfection! Add to that: clean toilets, rapid and cheerful service, and a strong free WiFi—we're very glad we took the detour!

There's another 13.4 kilometres (plus 600 metre!) to Santiago from here—we take the precaution of reserving an albergue whilst we have the Internet (another discussion!)—this guarantees us somewhere to stay tonight but also commits us to arriving today . . . we've had nearly an hour here, resting and eating—time to go!

More country, more woodland, and slowly but surely, more houses, roads, people—but NO open bars! On the Camino anyway!

It seems endless, with unceasing ups and downs. We cheer ourselves on by remembering how we made it up O Faro.

A cooling stream under a tiny Roman bridge gives our hot feet some much-needed respite. Mojons bearing the kilometres left to go have reappeared. Each promises a shorter distance than the one before, but the decrease seems agonisingly slow. I begin to worry that the 9:00 p.m. deadline for arrival at the albergue won't be met . . . and start not to care as my energy and enthusiasm wanes.

FINALLY! Just after 4:00 p.m., the towers of Santiago cathedral come into view between houses on the outskirts of the city.

For a lot of yesterday and today I've been physically aware of a subtle, magnetic pull this city, with her cathedral heart, has been exerting on me, drawing me again into her multicultural midst.

There's a final, small sting in the tail of the Invierno—the last road up to the old centre, entering from this direction, is incredibly steep! We look at it, laugh, and get on with the job.

When we walk into the Plaza Obradoiro at exactly 5:00 p.m., my sense is that not a lot is different to when I walked in a little under two years' ago. Certainly, there's a mix of pilgrims and tourists mingling together, street buskers (some playing the same sort of music in the same place!) and the cathedral is still wrapped and scaffolded for cleaning!

In exactly twenty-four hours we leave, having completed our pilgrim journey with all the obligatory observances—a celebratory meal, visit to the pilgrim office for our Compostela (this was nearly refused due to a day of missing stamps when we climbed O Faro), and the midday pilgrim Mass, where the swinging of the Botafumeiro delights me as always.

After my first Camino I told friends that I had walked Spain into my heart. I am so grateful to have renewed this very special connection through the Camino de Invierno.

Buen camino!
Bronwyn Cole July, 2017.

The Stray Dog AKA Bruno

By J. P. Vincent

"He's in the middle of the road, stupid dog," I thought to myself, as I drove the long uphill climb on the way home. The dog in question was "Bruno," a young, about two years old, cream and white Spanish Mastine. I stopped the car and he loped over, wagging his long, ungainly tail, sign of happiness apparently, a great big sign that commenced at the base of his spine and, before reaching the tip, another had already started its journey, creating a serpentine shimmy. Mastines aren't built for excitability. They're too big and lumbering. I suppose the best description of his gait is a gentle lollop, a sort of rolling canter, but in slow motion. "Come on you, get in the back of the car. You're coming home with me." I couldn't leave him there. All sorts of possibilities with terrible consequences kept coming to mind. He heaved himself onto the back seat. This was the second time for him and he was used to the car by now.

As our house was only about 3 kilometres away, I didn't think he would be a problem. He hung his head out of one open back window and his tail extended through the other, still gently swishing back and forth. "Good boy. We'll get home and get you something to eat." I like conversations with dogs because they seem to understand me. I shut my door, put on my seatbelt, checked the mirror, indicated, and pulled out. Old habits die hard even on the narrow, empty back roads of Galicia.

I checked my mirror once more, just in case, and behind me appeared from nowhere a dark blue national police car. "Where on earth did he come from," I wondered. He overtook me, spun round, and stopped. "I think I'd better stop," I said to Bruno, who seemed to agree with another wag. Both policemen got out and strode toward me.

Now, remember the following conversation was in Spanish, and as my Spanish isn't perfect, this is what I believe was said.

"Is this your dog?" Hands on hips and a serious demeanour.

"No."

"Why did you put him in the car?"

"Because he was wandering along the middle of the road."

"Do you know him?"

"Yes." And this is where the conversation became complicated. I did know him.

About three weeks previously he appeared in our garden and ate all the cat's food. He was a bit thin but healthy. He must have belonged to someone, a very handsome sociable dog with no injuries or outward signs of ill treatment, and looking at him he wasn't a cross-breed— not that I'm an expert.

This I tried to explain to the younger, more forceful policeman. Unfortunately, I didn't make myself clear and he asked me another question, which I didn't understand. He asked the question several times, his voice harsher, louder and more rapid with each repetition. My eyes started to prickle. Please not now, not in front of two of Spain's finest boys in blue.

Another question and this one I did understand "I.D. Where's your I.D.? And the documents for the car?"

It gets worse. I didn't have any I.D. I'd come out for a few minutes to run an errand, leaving my purse containing my N.I.E. and drivers licence on the kitchen table ready to pick up on my way out. The documents for the car were, thankfully, in the car. He seemed satisfied with these. My prickling eyes were leaking.

"Are you the dog's owner?"

"No. He was eating all our cat's food and we fed him," I tried to explain to younger policeman. "But we don't have secure fencing and he wandered off during the night."

When Bruno, we call him this but we have no idea of his real name, arrived three weeks ago. we fed him the scraps from our lunch and a few cat biscuits. That evening, after shopping, we fed him dried dog food, which he chomped through in seconds. And it looked like he was going to stay.

We posted his photo on Facebook and via Amarcan, a local dog rescue site, asking for any information about his owners. Nothing came forth. We contacted a local vet to see if he was chipped, but they were on holiday.

The following day I fed Bruno the dried dog food. He sniffed it once, tipped over the bowl with a paw, turned tail and walked off over our stone wall, and disappeared for several hours. When he returned, he would only eat the scraps from our lunch and the cat biscuits. The next day he disappeared once again, and we spent a couple of hours searching for him, without success.

We met him a few days later wandering along the same stretch of road near the breakers yard, alone and quite happy. We bundled him into the back of the car a leg at a time. We worried he would cause an accident and be injured. It was hard work lifting just a quarter of seventy-to-eighty kilos of dog, especially one that had probably never been in a car before and had no idea what we were trying to do. We took him to the Guarda Civil in Monforte de Lemos, our nearest town, to see if they had a chip reader. No, it was out on patrol—not literally, just in the patrol car. We went up to anther vet, and she checked for a chip. No, he didn't have one, and we asked her what we should do. She replied that, officially, as he didn't have an registered owner, we could keep him. We were excited. We thought he was gorgeous and would suit us very well—an outdoor, independent dog, not overly energetic, and good company. We would fix the fencing to keep him in. Many Mastines are chained, but it wasn't the route we wanted to take.

We took him home and locked him in the workshop, with a bed and plenty of food and water. It was only temporary. We watched videos that night on how to walk a dog on a lead—Cesar Milan, you're amazing—and it looked very simple. Next day, with a long leash attached to his chain collar, we set about walking with him. After about fifteen to twenty minutes, he was walking to heel beautifully. We let him off the lead and he remained at heel. We've cracked it, we thought. We turned into our lane and up to the house, looked round, and he'd gone! We saw him, or rather his tail held high, across the other side of the valley following another couple with their dog, and he was beautifully at heel.

Back to the story. The second policeman, a kind, fatherly figure of a man, wandered over to the nearby breakers yard and returned with a grease-covered lad. The breakers was where Bruno wandered off to after leaving us. The lad was very concerned by how upset I was and thought it was because I wanted the dog. In part, it was, but the reality of the situation was we could never keep such an independent dog on our property. Whereas, the breakers was well fenced and he would have company all day every day.

"He has an owner?" younger policeman queried.

"I don't know, but he isn't chipped."

"How do you know he isn't chipped?" And I explained, or I thought I had, about our visit to the Guardia and subsequent visit to a local vet. The young grease-covered man looked very worried and tried out his English and asked if I wanted the dog. The policeman insisted Bruno belonged to the breakers, and the prickling behind my eyes had become a silent slither of tears, which in turn steamed up my glasses and all objects in front of me became a blur.

It was turning out to be one of those days where I should have not got up in the first place. Firstly, I'd been helping with some fencing at the stables because the horses had escaped and I managed to get sunburnt. Secondly, after the emergency fencing repairs I'd gone home, cut a cover for a chair, and after several hours work made one cut too many and ruined the whole piece. So, I felt fragile. And now finding Bruno wandering along the middle of the road and my being accused of dognapping. These events and the younger policeman's manner caused the tears to flow.

With blurred vision and a runny nose, I phoned John, whose Spanish is far better than mine. Through my sobs and hiccoughs, I told him what had happened. He explained to the policeman what we'd done with the dog, how we knew him, and why we did what we did.

The policeman informed me that he wasn't going to fine me for not having any I.D. or for picking up a dog that wasn't mine and that, in his opinion, the owners of the dog were the breakers. And in future, if I find another stray, I am to call the police. It is one of their jobs after all.

Bruno, probably not his new name, is very happy at the breakers yard. He has company from eight till eight every day and lots of attention. The evidence is his black greasy ruff from constant caresses and his concrete coated coat from where he sleeps on the ground, as he did at ours even though we made him a very large, comfortable bed. And there's his great head on the counter and his long serpentine waggy tail when he sees anyone coming. Lastly, his joy at having a different choice of food every day from the men's lunches.

The moral to this tale is, in Spain always carry I.D., even if only going out to run an errand. And if you see a dog wandering or looking lost or eating your cat's food, don't rescue it. Phone the police. And, finally, if you're having a bad day, admit it, go back to bed, and start again the following morning.

FICTION

The "Santa Compaña"

By Noelia Roca Jones

I remember when I was a child, at the age of eleven or twelve, I loved spending time at my grandmother's house. Her house was in a village called Santa Mariña del Monte, which was full of trees, a lot of beautiful flowers . . . and you could hear the sound of animals. I loved playing in the fields, feeding the chickens, and walking up the mountain with my dogs while I looked for blackberries to use in a delicious cake. But, the best thing that I really loved was, during the summer nights, sitting on the balcony with a hot chocolate and looking at the sky, without clouds but full of stars, and hearing the sound of a night bird like the owl.

But one night, a strange thing happened. That night wasn't a typical relaxing and peaceful night. The atmosphere was tense and gloomy and it made me feel a strange emotion somewhere between anxiety and fear.

I was sitting like every evening, when suddenly I heard the sound of a lot of little bells and voices murmuring something that sounded like prayers in the distance. Immediately, I ran into the house and looked for a torch and decided to go back out and find out what was happening and what the voices were, but without going too far. When I found the source of the sounds, at that moment, I was paralysed and I couldn't move. I couldn't believe my eyes!

What was that? A slight smell like a burnt candle invaded the path in front of my grandmother's house. I saw something strange, like people dressed in black tunics without shoes. They were each carrying a candle. I was sure that the strange smell came from those candles. I was really scared, so I went back home, closed the doors and windows, and tried to switch on the television and forget what I had seen. But I couldn't forget the strange fear that I was feeling.

The next day, when I went to my father's house, I told him what had happened and I could see how his face changed completely. He knew what I was talking about. He asked me if these people had seen me, and I answered that they hadn't. Then, he hugged me really tightly and I didn't understand what had actually happened. He told me to sit on the sofa, and he began to explain that the people who I had seen were "La Santa Compaña".

The legend is that about twice a year, on Halloween (the night of the 31st of October) and on Midsummer's Night (the night of 23rd of June), you can find the "Santa Compaña" wandering during the night. The "Santa Compaña" is formed by two lines of spectres, and in each line, there are eight spectres. They are souls in Purgatory who wear a black tunic and carry a bone with a light at the top of it like a candle. The procession is guided by a living person who carries a cross and a candle. They walk praying, normally rosaries, singing funeral songs, and making the little bells ring. You can feel their presence because suddenly cold air is felt, you can hear an absolute silence, and you smell the burning candles that invade the paths and streets where the "Santa Compaña" passes. Animals are frightened and run away while dogs howl, announcing their arrival.

The living person who guides the "Santa Compaña" can be a man or a woman. The person doesn't remember anything of what happened the night before, but people can recognise that person because of their extreme thinness and paleness. Every night their light will burn more intensely but their face will be more pallid. The person can't rest, so every day they will be weaker until they become seriously ill, and people won't know the reason. The person will be condemned to wander every night until their death or until another person is surprised by the "Santa Compaña". Then, the person who guides the procession will give them the cross and the candle which they carry during the procession. If you are a witness of the "Santa Compaña's" passing, you will be given the cross and your soul will be dragged to the world of the dead. Only the children who were baptised by a priest who used the oil of the deceased, will have the power to see the "Santa Compaña" when they are adults.

Its appearance announces the unavoidable death of a person in a few days. The procession also appears to reproach living people for the mistakes they have made. If the person has made a grave mistake, this person will be visited by the "Santa Compaña" and become the guide of the procession and they will be obliged to wander until another living person replaces them.

If the story is told, this will be good to protect people from the "Santa Compaña". There are some rites to protect oneself against it, too. When the person gives you the cross, you will have to open your arms and say the words "Jesus Christ". When the living person who guides the procession tells you. "It's your turn" or "Here you are", you should reply, "I have a cross". You can also protect yourself if you cross your arms when you are walking or if you fill your hands with stones and sticks. The "Santa Compaña" won't have the power to sweep your soul along to the world of the dead if at that moment you are standing next to a "Cruceiro", which is a big stone cross in the middle of a crossroad, or if at that moment, you are carrying a cross and you have enough time to show it. You will also be able to protect yourself against it if you draw a circle around you on the floor while the procession is going by. The protection will be increased if the circle that you draw on the floor is made of an olive branch and inside it you draw a pentacle (a five-pointed star). Another option could be to run away.

When my father finished telling me the legend, I investigated in the village if anybody had died a few days ago. However, to my surprise, two days later, an old person who lived near my grandmother died. He was eight-nine years old and he was very ill and hadn't too much time left. At that moment, I was lost for words. I couldn't believe it. I thought, "What would have happened if I had run into the "Santa Compaña"? Would I be the one who replaced the living person and would I be the guide who led the procession while carrying the cross and the candle every night?" After that day, I changed completely. I avoided going out at night, and if I had to do it, I always carried a little cross with me.

I had never asked myself why there are big stone crosses in the middle of the crossroad. I thought they were built because the people who lived in a nearby village were Christian and the crosses were a beautiful symbol of this. But the crosses aren't there by coincidence. The crosses are there to protect people from the "Santa Compaña".

A lot of pilgrims who go along the Route to Santiago will find these symbols and will think the crosses are exciting monuments, but the real reason is that they are there to protect them from something strange and terrifying.

When I was investigating about the stories of "Santa Compaña", I found out that in a village called "Rías Baixas" there were many people who had met this famous procession.

My story happened about thirteen years ago, but even nowadays, if I have to go out late at night, I carry a little cross with me.

Guerrillas Come in Many Different Shapes

By Robin Hillard

Our teachers did not understand the Napoleonic Wars. At school we learned about Trafalgar and Wellington, with some mention of Russia, but my brothers and I knew what really brought the Corsican general down because we learned our history in Josefina's kitchen.

Dad said Josefina came from Spain, but she tossed her head proudly and told us she was born in Galicia. "My land is called Galicia, no matter what that Franco says," and our ladylike neighbour spat at Franco's name. My mother explained that Galicia is one of a number of little kingdoms in the country we call Spain and that General Franco won a war that gave him control over them all.

Josefina's parents were killed in the first terrible days of the Civil War and she had been sent, with a boatful of young refugees, to Britain. She grew up, married an Irishman, and came with him to the dusty goldfields of Western Australia, where, to our delight, she lived next door.

My brothers and I would sit in Josefina's kitchen while she told us about her rainy, green Galicia. She talked about witches and saints as if they were as much part of the community as the greengrocer or baker. We learned about the Moors, who had conquered most of Spain "but not our brave Galicia". Those invaders had been repulsed by Galician fighters led by St Peter himself, the saint whose bones lay in the cathedral of Santiago de Compostela. He came riding on his great white horse to lead the battle against the Moors. I dreamed about that great white horse.

I also dreamed about the brave Maria Pita from Coruna, who chased Sir Francis Drake out of the town. Josefina waved her carving knife to show how Maria grabbed the sword of a dead soldier and led her townsfolk against the English sailors.

My brothers were fascinated by tales of ships, loaded with gold, that were wrecked off the Galician "Coast of Death". They spent hours swimming and diving in the local pool, preparing for the day when they could go to Galicia and hunt for that treasure.

Those were all grand stories, but most of all we liked to hear about the Galician peasants who chased Napoleon's army out of Spain.

"When they didn't have guns, those peasants," Josefina said, "they fought with anything they could hold. They cut branches off the trees to throw at the soldiers and rolled huge rocks down the sides of the mountains to crush the French troops. There were no telephones, so officers in charge of the French battalions had to send each other messages. Our men attacked the mounted messengers, so they could not deliver their letters and none of the officers knew what the others were doing."

Josefina's eyes flashed when she talked about the ragged men who overcame impossible odds to defeat Napoleon's Grande Armee and destroy the Great French Empire.

"That's not exactly true," Dad said dryly, when Billy repeated the boast. "The Russians and English were also in that war."

Who cared about the Russians and English? The next day we trooped into Josefina's kitchen and begged to hear about the "great French army," though Billy nearly spoiled the story by repeating Dad's comment.

"Maybe not the whole French army," Josefina admitted. "There was fighting all over Europe. But Napoleon sent his best fighter, the great Marshal Ney, to Galicia, and we chased him out of the country."

She told us how badly the French behaved in Spain. Because Napoleon had to pay for his expensive war, he tried to get money from the conquered land. His soldiers pillaged our churches. They loaded their carts with our precious plate and ornaments to melt them down for gold, but their looting did not help the emperor. Our men watched from the mountains, and when they saw the soldiers with their carts, the peasants leapt down on them like wolves attacking a deer."

There were no mountains in our yard, so my brothers had to jump off the roof of the shed when they fought the French army. Our cat was terrified by the first assault, but she soon got used to the noise and watched the brave guerrillas from a safe distance. The neighbourhood stray was less blasé and fled like Marshal Ney's men.

I did not share these games, but when Josefina's daughter, little Rosalia, tucked her dolls into their bed on the veranda, I promised to keep them safe from Marshal Ney and the Emperor Napoleon.

Rosalia had been named for the wonderful poet, Rosalia de Castro, whose words Josefina sang, in the lilting notes of a remembered language, followed by words we could understand. She chased away our childish fears with an incantation to the morning.

Depart, night start fleeing!
Come, dawn, start breaking
With your face that smiling
Scares away the shadow!

The shadows of my world were horrible sums with fractions that had to be multiplied or divided according to the whim of an otherwise kind teacher. Who cared what happened when 5/6 was divided by 7/8? Much as I loved Josefina's songs I felt it would take more than the morning sun to brighten the gloom of those awful numbers.

"It's impossible," I said, one afternoon, scrubbing at the recalcitrant figures till my eraser tore a hole in the page.

Josefina did not agree. "Nothing is impossible, Betsy." she said. "Didn't our people beat the French army? Maybe not the whole French army." she admitted again, sharing that glory with the English Duke, "but our people made the French retreat. The Guerrilla fighters in Galicia were like the numbers in your times tables that help with those horrible sums."

I wanted to hear more about guerrillas beating the French army and forget about the sums that always came out wrong.

"Maybe you're just stupid," Billy teased.

"No, you are not stupid, little Betsy," Josefina said fiercely. "That's what the great French marshal said about our men. Our people were poor, and the French soldiers despised them because they were in rags, not like the uniforms of Ney's men, with their smart red, white, and blue. One officer sneered at our fighters because 'they spend their afternoons raising animals and ploughing.' As if working in the fields made men dumb and slow. Ney was sure his experienced soldiers would defeat those ragged ones, but he soon learned to be frightened of our men.

"Napoleon called Galicia 'the Spanish Ulcer,' but if we were a sickness for the French, we were medicine for Spain, a medicine that saved the whole country. Like the times tables will save you, when you do your sums."

I felt that last sentence spoiled the story. Could anything be more boring than times tables?

"Your tables are no duller than nights in the mountains," Josefina said. "Waiting waiting, war is mostly waiting. Our men stayed out in the cold, among the jagged rocks." she hunched over the table, shivering like a guerrilla hiding behind the rocks. "They would rather have been sitting by the fire in a warm kitchen, just as you would rather be outside playing instead of sitting in your classroom doing sums.

"But like you with your schoolwork, they did not give up. Just as you struggle to learn your seven times six, they persevered. They positioned themselves in the mountains and threw rocks down on the enemy. When they didn't have guns, they attacked the French with rakes and hoes and pointed sticks."

Fired by thoughts of the peasants, I fought my own war with the sums. Every correct answer was a victory to be celebrated in Josefina's kitchen, every cross on my page a temporary defeat, like the first advances of Napoleon's army that, as Josefina said, "did them no good in the end."

The day I came home with a page full of ticks she repeated Wellington's speech as he left Galicia, telling his soldiers to "Strive all of you to imitate the inimitable Gallegans. Let their intrepidity be remembered to the end of the world, for it has never been surpassed . . ." "So nothing is impossible," she said, flourishing my victorious page.

"What happened after the war?" Billy asked, eager for more stories.

"After the war," Josefina said sadly, "the big men in Madrid brought the old world back. Our Galicia was swallowed by the Central government. Our language was considered inferior to the tongue of Castile and our culture submerged by that of greater Spain.

"But people from Galicia will never give up," she said, tossing her head. "Guerrillas come in many different shapes, and there's more than one way to win the war." She reached into a drawer to pull out a bundle of letters, which she spread over the table so we could see the South American stamps. "The families of those ragged peasants, who chased Napoleon out of our country, many of them had to leave their land. But they are still Gallego. They've carried our culture across the ocean and kept our language alive."

They might be scattered to the corners of the globe, but as we children listened to Josefina we knew the exiles dreamed of Galicia just as Josefina, with her stories, brought Galicia to our goldfields home.

"Guerrillas come in many different shapes," Josefina said again. "Like your times tables sneaking into sums, our people will sneak into the Spanish government." I puffed out my chest, as if my small victory was proof that Josefina's Galicia would never be submerged by a central government. "We defeated the French and one day we will be able to walk proudly again in our beautiful Galicia, and our streets will ring with her tongue."

Thanks to Josefina, I started to see myself as "good at school" and even became a teacher. Children still had to multiply, and in a pre-decimal Australia their sums included shillings and pence as well as the hated fractions, but Josefina with her tales of Marshal Ney was an unseen presence in my classroom. Her stories about "Guerrillas fighting in the hills like times tables sneaking into sums," appealed to my students as they had to me.

Like most Australian girls, both Rosalia and I spent a few years travelling, but neither of us would visit Franco's Spain. Rosalia has raised her own daughter on Josefina's stories and we are both delighted that Jacqui is travelling in Galicia. A Galicia that triumphantly proclaims its own identity with a language that is taught in schools and proudly spoken in the street. The region has its own parliament, the Xunta, that writes its rules in the Galician tongue.

Jacqui remembered my fascination with Marshal Ney. When she was in Pontevedra she visited the site of the battle of Sampayo Bridge, and took a picture of the river, together with one in the city, of a monument dedicated to the heroes of that battle. I have printed them out on glossy paper and pinned them to my study notice board. So, whenever I get disheartened by the daily grind, I can think of those ragged fighters who chased the French army out of their country and tell myself that sometimes we can do the impossible.

~

NOTES:

As Betsy's father pointed out, the downfall of Napoleon was not entirely due to Galicia. Other nations did play some part in the defeat of the little Corsican. And you will find a more nuanced description of the guerrillas contribution to the Peninsular wars, and their influence on future conflict at

https://www.napoleon.org/en/history-of-the-two-empires/articles/bleeding-ulcer-the-commencement-and-long-term-consequences-of-guerilla-warfare-in-iberia/

You will find an account of the Battle of the Sampayo Bridge at the Spanish website

201406021646.htmlthttp://www.abc.es/archivo/20 140603/abci-batalla-puente-sampayo-201406021646.htm,

which Google will kindly translate for Anglophones.

If you want to read some of the poetry Josefina loved, Eduardo Freire Canosa has very generously put his translations of Rosalia de Castro's poems into the public domain at http://rosaliadecastropoems.esy.es/#Poem1.

What Colour Is Your Tractor?

By Gary Gaunt

I've lived in Galicia for six years now, but something has just struck me: nearly all of the tractors are red. Javier, the farmer in our village, has two large tractors, both red. Suso, the farmer in the next village, also has two large tractors, both red. Antonio, the man in the house at the top of the village, has a small brand-new tractor: red.

I could go on, but have a look for yourself; tractors in Galicia are almost all red. Why is that? It isn't a company colour, like, for example, Ferrari—there are many different makes, but seemingly only one colour—red. Perhaps it's a bit like hand tools: axes and sickles and so on. Most of them have a painted bit (often red), so it's easy to locate them when you're working in the woods or the fields. I'm sure this is the reason, and a story I heard recently supports my theory.

A man with a green tractor was working in his field when his dog suddenly ran off into the nearby woodland, baying furiously. The man, not wishing to miss an opportunity, grabbed his shotgun and gave chase. After twenty minutes both man and dog gave up the chase and headed back to the tractor. The tractor? After a further twenty minutes searching he finally located his camouflaged vehicle. The man returned home and painted red stripes down both sides. He's never lost it since.

So, that's one theory. But there are others. What if, many years ago, a clerk at Massey Ferguson was typing up an order for 10,000 gallons of red paint when a lapse of concentration caused him to type an extra couple of zeros? They haven't run out yet!

I know that by now many of you will be thinking, 'Hold on a minute, John Deere tractors are green.' And this is true, but back to my theory. Imagine a man running frantically up and down fields and hillsides, staring into the distance, worried and perspiring. 'What's the problem?'

'I can't find my tractor.'

'When did you last see it?'

'About an hour ago. My dog chased a wild boar into the woods and I followed.'

'Is your tractor a John Deere, by any chance?'

'Yes, it is. How did you know?'

'Oh, just a guess. Would you like to buy some red paint?'

'Que?'

So, the theory's looking good—nobody makes green footballs, do they?

A thought has just occurred to me: Is that why Ferrari don't make tractors? Think about it, if you spotted a low-slung, sleek red sports car a hundred metres away, you'd know it was a Ferrari. If you were sitting by the roadside having a bottle of Estrella and a cheese butty, and a low-slung, sleek red car flew past you at 150 kilometres per hour, you'd know it was a Ferrari. Now bear with me on this. If Ferrari made tractors and you saw one from a hundred metres away, it would look just like any other tractor. Or, if you were sitting by the roadside having a bottle of Estrella and a cheese butty and a large red tractor ambled by, you probably wouldn't even give it a cursory glance. It's just another red tractor. That's why Ferrari don't make tractors—no kudos, no great impression, no 'Wow!' factor. See what I mean?

Red, of course, has always been a danger colour: road signs, traffic lights, flags—all the red ones offer you a warning, thus presenting us with theory number two.

Perhaps the reason tractors are red: It's a warning—it's big, it's heavy, it would drive over your Fiat 500 without the driver even noticing. But then again, elephants are grey . . .

Off at a tangent here for a moment. You don't see as many red cars on the road as you used to, do you? Why is that, do you think? Here's an idea. Let's say Jose has just bought a brand spanking new red BMW. He stops at the local bar for a bottle of Estrella and a cheese butty, and in walk a crowd of his friends. He listens with interest to the story of Javi losing his John Deere tractor, and then says proudly, 'Hey, boys, I've just collected my new Bimmer, come and take a look!'

Everyone shuffles outside and he proudly points to his gleaming new car. 'What do you think, boys?'

They look at the car. They walk round it. They stroke it.

'Well,' he repeats. 'What do you think?'

'It's the same colour as Pablo's tractor.'

'Yes, but . . .'

'And the tractor of Luis.'

'Yes, but . . .'

'And Antonio's tractor is the same colour.'

They turn and go back into the bar, leaving Jose staring into space despondently. His pride and joy has been demoted to the league of tractors, and why? Because it's red!

If the tractor was a faster beast (actually, much faster) it would make the perfect getaway vehicle for bank robberies. Imagine the police interviewing witnesses:

'Sir, did you see the getaway vehicle?'

'Yes, I did.'

'What was it?'

'A tractor.'

'What type?'

'Red.'

'Any idea of the make?'

'Oh, I don't know . . . a red one—they all look the same to me.'

Back at Police Headquarters they set about tracking down a red tractor. The tractor database tells them there are 10,000 possibilities. Thirty of the first forty questioned as to their whereabouts at the time of the robbery say they were helping a neighbour look for his John Deere.

Incidentally, whilst we're back to John Deere for a moment, you obviously know that the Guardia Civil vehicles are painted green? But what you probably didn't know is that each vehicle emits a digital signal and that every policeman carries a small handheld tracking device, a bit like a mobile phone. The reason? Well, should the Guardia be in hot pursuit of a souped-up red tractor fleeing with the contents of the safe of the local bank, and should that tractor drift off the road into the countryside, and should the Guardia get stuck and have to pursue on foot, the tracking device will assist them in locating their green vehicle (which by now has probably been run into by a red tractor looking for a lost John Deere!).

Wild Horses

By Olivia Stowe

"Remember to refill the water trough in the south pasture."

Well, thanks, Sis, I would never have thought of doing that for the thirtieth time in a row this month if you hadn't reminded me." The porch door banged shut so loudly behind Alec that the four women sitting around the porch table jumped. Vicky looked down at the table and the other three women shared brief meaningful looks before going back to sipping drinks and assembling brochures for Sinclair Horse Ranch boarding stables in the lush, rolling hills to the southwest of Lexington, Virginia.

"So, how's the arrangement with your cute brother to come help you run the ranch working out?" Denise, a Lexington Realtor and a recent divorcee—for the third time—with a roving eye, asked with a straight face.

"He's not cute, and don't you dare do your vamp thing on him," Victoria—Vicky to her friends—Sinclair, their hostess, answered, giving her friend a mock glaring stare. "And we're doing just fine."

"Certainly sounds that way," Denise said, with a snort.

"Stop picking on her, and I saw Alec first," the redhead at the table, Peggy Cooper, said.

Denise Lee, the curvy bottle blond, snorted again and said, "Fat chance that would do either of you any good." She gave a meaningful look at the fourth, raven-haired, voluptuous Spanish woman at the table, Sabela Rios. That Peggy and Sabela, who jointly owned a gift shop in Lexington, which stocked quite a few selections from

Sabela's native Galician, northwest Spain, region of origin, were a couple was known and comfortably accommodated by both Vicky and Denise.

In turn, the couple joked with Denise about her propensity to chase, catch, use, and release men and were supporting Vicky through her bereavement. Vicky had lost her husband to a tragic fall from a horse that early spring. Four years earlier, Vicky and John Sinclair had opened a sanctuary ranch for ill-treated horses, where, in addition to boarding and training horses, they brought derelict horses back to health. As a hallmark of and advertisement for the ranch, the Sinclairs had teamed horses they rehabilitated to sleekness to pull an old Western-style stagecoach through Lexington's streets in its Fourth of July Parade the last three years. Their friends, Peggy and Sabela and Denise and whatever man she was matched with that year, joined the Sinclairs in dressing in Old West attire to ride on the stage coach.

The bond between these people had grown deep and they'd all been devastated by John's death earlier that year. July 4th was fast approaching again, and Vicky's three friends had been discussing what to do about the Fourth of July Parade. Thus far it had been obvious to all of them that Vicky wasn't emotionally up to doing that again—at least not this year. It had been John's favorite activity and, because it was his, Vicky had taken it as hers too. Her brother, Alec Gleason, had come to help her out with the ranch, and they were doing all right there, but Vicky just wasn't regaining the spark she once had. At the same time she was clutching at what she still had, which wasn't helpful when there was more work to do than one person could physically manage alone.

As was usual, after the topic had been talked around today but not yet directly tackled, it was Denise who plowed into it. "It's June, Vicky. What were you thinking about doing with the Fourth of July Parade this year?"

"Well, I don't know . . . I haven't given it much—"

"Because Peggy and Sabela won't be able to ride with the stage coach this year, if you were thinking of taking it out and spinning it around downtown. Did Sabela tell you? They're going to a festival in Spain—in the La Estrada region in Galicia, near where Sabela was born—and including a buying spree for stock for the gift shop. I'm thinking of going with them. We . . . I think you should think about doing that too. It would be good for you to get away. I know the July 4th weekend will be hard on you."

"Oh, I couldn't possible get away. The ranch—"

". . . Would be just fine with Alec running it for a while," Denise continued. "It would be good for both of you to separate for a bit. That little set to the two of you had just now about filling a water trough is what made me think of it."

That, of course, was one big fib. The women and Alec had gotten together on this point already.

"You need time away from all of this, and Alec needs to be alone with it for a while for you both to accept that he can handle it, so that both of you will feel comfortable to pull away from it for a few days from time to time."

"Well, I don't know . . . I don't think—"

"Here. Here's a brochure on the hotel we're going to in Galicia," Sabela said on cue, taking a couple of pamphlets out of her purse and fanning them out on the table. "Isn't it great—with that ancient building ruin below the hotel by the pool, with its roof open to the stars and used for open dining? And here's information on the festival. It's an old one, symbolic of going from childhood to adulthood—"

"Ah, a sex rite," Denise interjected, with a laugh.

"Down girl," Sabela said. "It's about horses. Wild horses. Bringing them down from the mountains once a year, checking them for healthiness, ID chipping them, cutting their manes and tails, and branding the foals. They make a three-day celebration out of it."

"Culling the wild horse herds and seeing to their needs?" Vicky asked, showing interest at last and picking up the brochure on the festival.

"Taking care of the horses, like you do here," Peggy said.

"That reminds me of John and how we met," Vicky said. "You know about the wild horses of Chincoteague Island, don't you, over on the Virginia coast?—that every year they have a festival of fording the wild ponies across to the mainland, checking them over, and moving some of them on to domestication, with human owners."

The other three wagged their heads, without committing to how much they knew about that—which was pretty much everything Vicky had in her memories. Alec had told them the story and they were using it now to try to bring their friend back into life.

"One summer," Vicky continued, "I was working in a gift shop on the mainland there and John was one of the young men herding the horses over the stretch of water they had to ford. I went out to watch the annual horse swim. The first time I saw John he was riding bareback on one of these Chincoteague ponies, guiding it to the mainland. He looked so handsome—fit and brown as a berry—and happy. Afterward he came into the gift shop and we talked about the wild horses. We discovered we both wanted to save horses from neglect. Matched interests, just like that. Imagine that."

"Yep, imagine that," Denise said with a straight face. "And so you two went right out and did the deed?"

"On a beach later that night after we'd visited the corral where they were keeping ponies that had been swum over that day and I saw how good he was at handling horses, yes," Vicky answered, "but that's all I have to say about that."

"Yes, who could possibly deny a fit, brown-as-a-berry man who played with wild horses?" Denise quipped, for which Vicky rewarded her by sticking her tongue out at her.

"Well, think about it—about going to Spain with us for the first weekend in July and taking in this festival," Peggy said, moving in to change the subject, her voice gentle and coaxing. "Sabela and I would like all of us to be together again for the Fourth of July—but the usual parade here in Lexington might be just too much to cope with this year. And we'll be gone and can't help you with it, and—"

"Well, I don't know," Vicky said.

"Keep these brochures to look at. We have another set," Sabela said.

Denise opened her mouth to speak again, but Peggy gave her a warning look, conveying that they had planted the seed as well as they could at this point and Denise's continued direct approach might not have the desired effect. Denise wisely snapped her jaw shut.

An hour later, Alec returned from the south pasture and found Vicky sitting alone on the porch, reading through the travel brochures.

"It's done as you commanded, Lord and Master," he said. "The horses in the south pasture have water. I told them to be grateful to you—that'd I'd just let them die of thirst myself, of course."

"I'm sorry I snapped at you," Vicky said. "But it's hard to let loose of the responsibilities around here. I'll try to be better. I know you're capable of doing it all."

"You know what we need," Alec said, acting like he'd just thought of it, even though he'd carefully worked it out with Denise, Peggy, and Sabela.

"No, what?"

"What we need is for you to take a vacation. It would do you a world of good and I'd have a chance to establish that I can handle the work around here—that I can hold up John's end. If you just weren't here for a few days, we'd both learn something. You'd learn to trust me to do my part and I'd learn whether there was something I needed to get a better handle on."

"A vacation? Maybe just a few days?" Vicky mused, fingering the brochures on the hotel and festival in Galicia. "Maybe you're right."

Alec damn well knew he was right—and so did Denise, Peggy, and Sabela.

* * * *

The dishes had been cleared away from the meal in the ancient, roofless stone-building ruin by the pool below the Torre do Rio Hotel in Galicia's Caldas de Reis, a town where they were staying in preparation to go to the start of the A Rapa das Bestas festival, the festival of the gathering of the wild horses, in the mountains near the town of Sabucedo the next day. Brandy had been brought, and a handsome, well-built Spanish man in his late thirties or early forties was playing the guitar and singing quietly in a deep, smooth baritone. His songs had been more lively during dinner, during which he kept looking over at the table the four women sat at and, Vicky imagined, mostly at her. She focused on him more now, with the meal done, because his songs had turned softer, more sensual. She did an assessment on him again; there wasn't a single test of appreciation that he didn't pass without further research and exposure.

"Isn't his singing divine?" Vicky turned to Denise and said. But Denise was only half listening to her. She was looking at a young, sultry, and dark Spanish man at a nearby table. The two had been flirting with each other with their eyes for some time.

"Yes, he's divine," Denise said. But she wasn't talking about the guitarist.

"The mood of the songs has changed," Vicky said to Sabela, turning in her direction.

"He's singing ancient Galician love songs now," Sabela answered.

The three women who weren't openly flirting with the young man at the nearby table gave their full attention to the singing and guitar playing.

A dona que eu am'o e tenho por senhor
A dona que eu am' e tenho por senhor
Amostráde-mi-a, Deus, se vos en prazer for,
senón, dáde-mi a morte.
A que tenh' eu por lume destes olhos meus,
e por que choran sempre, amostráde-mi-ama, Deus,
senón, dáde-mi a morte.

"What is he singing, Sabela? Can you give me the gist?"

"Yes, of course. It's a love song by the thirteenth-century troubadour Bernal de Bonaval. That's according to the notes in Spanish I was given when we came in on what the guitarist would be singing tonight—his name is Uxio Silva, by the way. He's singing it in ancient Galician. It goes something like, 'That lady I love is my dear mistress. If it's your will, show her to me in all her beauty, God. If not, put me to death. And then something about her being the light of his eyes and for God to let him have her or do away with him."

"He looks like he's singing it directly to Vicky," Peggy said. She reached for Sabela's hand from affection— affected by the song and affection with Sabela.

"Yes, yes, it does," Sabela said, with a low laugh.

Vicky was about to say something—she was blushing—but just then the young Spanish man had risen from his table and was there beside their table, addressing

Denise in Spanish and giving her a look that suggested that he was looking forward to another dessert course.

"Gustaríache bailar comigo, fermosa?" the young man said, smiling at Denise and extending a hand toward her.

"What is he asking?" Denise queried of Sabela. She was gazing back at the young man, obviously drinking him in and liking everything she saw.

"He's begging you to dance with him. He's calling you a 'pretty lady' in Galician Spanish. But of course—"

"But of course I will dance with you," Denise said to the young man. She accompanied the young man to the terrace by the pool and they went into an immediate close clutch, swaying with and against each other. From the outset, saying they were dancing just seemed to be an excuse for what they really were interested in.

Whatever other spell was being woven at the table was broken, and Vicky rose and said, "Well, if we have to be in this village, Sabucedo, at seven in the morning, I, for one, need to get to bed." She was still blushing as she left.

The singing guitarists watched her go, and it wasn't lost on her as she ascended the several flights of stairs to the hotel proper above that he changed back to more lively music.

Back at the ruins, Peggy and Sabela also prepared to leave. Denise obviously wasn't going anywhere—at least not with them.

"Tell me, you didn't set that up, did you—between the guitarist and Vicky?" Peggy asked Sabela.

"No, certainly not. But it almost worked a charm, don't you think?"

"Well, it has certainly worked a charm with Denise," Peggy answered. "What are the chances she will be climbing the mountain to look for wild horses in the morning with us?"

"Close to something between zero and nil," Sabela said, with a snort.

* * * *

Despite being the first weekend in July, it was a bit chilly where they gathered in a small football stadium in the village of Sabucedo at 7:00 the next morning. There were only three of them, of course. Each had knocked on Denise's door at one time or other between 5:30 and when they'd gotten in the rental car to drive to Sabucedo, but none of them had done so with the expectation that Denise would accompanying them that day. They knew Denise all too well.

Others had gathered, as well—many others—for the walk up the nearby mountain. The English speakers had all been gathered together in one group and given instructions on what was to happen that day, which would end with the wild horses they'd rounded up on the mountain being held in a fenced-in area up there overnight and herded back down to this football stadium the next day for the A Rapa Das Bestas—mane-cutting and tagging—ceremony. All of those who had showed up for the festival would be divided into smaller, but still large, groups to gather horses at three different locations before the horses were herded to the mountain enclose.

Some of what was going to happen seemed to be unnecessary to Vicky and her companions, but the ceremony had been set in stone since at least the eighteenth century, with some saying it went back to the Bronze Age as a symbolic coming-of-age ritual, so there was no use making suggestions.

While accepting this, Peggy did say, "I guess it's good Denise didn't come along after all; she would have been trying to force logical change on all of this and undoubtedly would have gotten us sent back to Caldas de Reis in a sealed van."

"And into the arms of her young dancer from last night—" Sabela dropped in.

"And this morning," Vicky interjected.

"And being banished before we had to walk up the mountain would have been her plan all along," Peggy completed. The three laughed.

That's when they saw the handsome guitarist from the hotel the previous evening ride by on a magnificent white stallion. He greeted them in Spanish and gave them a smile as he continued on.

"Gorgeous," Peggy said in his wake.

"Yes, most of the riders milling around are on white horses, and several of them are as magnificent as that one is," Vicky said. "I wonder why there are so many white horses."

"You'll see when we find the group of wild horses we are to gather up," Sabela said. "The riders who herd them up, quiet them down, and guide them to the enclosure from our group will all be on white horses. It's something they are trying as an experiment this year. That is to make them more easily identified from the wild horses by the rest of us, and, theoretically, based on observations from recent years, the other horses seem to react better to guidance by white horses. Most of those horses once were wild too. If their observations pan out, I'm told they will separate the white ones out to train for future ceremonies."

"Interesting, but I was referring to the man, not the horse," Peggy said, with a giggle. The other two joined her in the laugh. Sabela and Peggy carefully refrained from looking at Vicky, who, yes, was blushing.

Once everyone was separated into groups and organized, they started the climb, by separate sylvan pathways under an enclosing canopy of trees, up onto the mountain. It wasn't lost to the three American women that the mounted guitarist—Uxio Silva—remained close to them as the three stayed together for the climb.

It wasn't long before they came across a herd of the wild horses, feeding in a rocky meadow about three-quarters of the way up the mountain. Silently, as they had been instructed, the people who were on foot fanned out around them, encircling them. The horses became skittish from the presence of the humans and started to move en masse—there were at least forty of them, eight or nine being young foals—in a circular motion. They wouldn't come close to a standing human nor try to move between them, so as the people moved into a loose circle, the horses moved in an arc—and into the control of the riders on the white horses.

The three American women were amazed by how simple and effective it had been to gather up the horses. Within the first couple of hours of the day, they had located a herd and in elegant, time-learned ways, the horses had permitted themselves to be pinned down and shunted into the line of white horses they permitted to guide them to a larger enclosure farther up on the mountain, where other groups were bringing in horses. By mid afternoon, well over 100 horses had been corralled on the mountain.

Locals were assigned to stay with them that night, while the rest went back down into the small village of Sabucedo, where a tent city had been set up around the football stadium—but not inside it—for a festival of food and music to be conducted for the evening and into the night. The playing field of the stadium was set up to receive the horses on the morrow, with a fenced corral, called a curro, being created there through the late afternoon and evening.

It wasn't the greatest surprise that Denise had arrived by the time the three women came down from the mountain or that she had in tow the young Spanish heartthrob who had wooed—and apparently been won by—her the previous evening. He was introduced to them as Anton Vasquez, a school teacher on summer break and not that long out of college himself—and, of course, nearly ten years younger than Denise was. That didn't seem to bother either of the two. With Sabela there now to translate, Anton and Denise had the opportunity to converse on an entirely, if probably not nearly as pleasant, a plane as they had been doing. He'd brought her from Caldas de Reis on a motorcycle, and she was glowing from the adventure of it all.

Vicky also glowed that night. The guitarist and singer, Uxio Silva, had also ridden back down the mountain on his white stallion for the night. Most of the riders stayed up at the mountain corral, but it soon became obvious that he'd come down because he was part of the festival entertainment. He played and sang into the wee hours of the morning, and, mesmerized by him, feeling he was singing directly to her—which he undoubtedly was—Vicky was lost in the magic of his deep baritone voice, the strumming of his guitar, and the silky sounds of Galician Spanish.

Sabela left the group for a few minutes and when she came back, she told them, "There are tents available if we want to overnight here rather than make the trek back and forth to the hotel. They say the horses will be brought down by eight tomorrow morning and the ceremony will start right away."

"I'm fine with staying, if others are," Peggy said, looking around for agreement.

"How big a tent should be we ask for?" Sabela asked, looking meaningfully at Denise. "For three or four?"

"Two, I would think," Denise answered. "Anton and I already have one reserved."

"Two?" Peggy asked.

"Yes, I would think Vicky has other arrangements too."

"Me?" Vicky asked, suddenly tearing her attention away from the music and looking surprised.

"Oh come on," Denise said. "You and Uxio have been making goo-goo eyes at each other since last night. It's time you let the charm and romance of Galicia take over and enjoyed yourself."

"Like you have?" Peggy asked, her voice amused.

"Damn right, like I have," Denise responded vehemently. "The greatest revenge in life is to live it fully. And you have your Galician beauty in Sabela. I have mine. Why can't Vicky let loose and have hers, as well?"

"A tent for three, please," Vicky turned to Sabela and said.

Denise snorted. "The romance of Galicia is going to get you yet, girl," she pronounced. "That's what fate has brought you here to discover."

No one responded to that, either to counter it or to push Vicky farther on what the other three had hoped this trip would produce.

* * * *

The next morning Vicky and the others were in the bleachers on one side of the football stadium as the riders on the white stallions herded the wild horses down from the mountain corral to the enclosure, the curro, on the playing field. After they had done so, pandemonium ruled for the next few hours as the festival of A Rapa das Bestas continued with, first, the separation of the foals from the rest of the horses so that they wouldn't be trampled in the melee that was then to proceed on the field. The men performing the ritual in the curro were called adoitadores. The foals were taken off to an adjacent enclosure, claimed by owners, and branded with the owners' brands and their manes cut and their tails docked.

The mature horses also had their manes and tails cut, but they had ID tags stapled inside their ears as well. The unique part of this exercise, though, was that the men inside the enclosure had to wrestle the horses into submission with only their body and bare hand strength for the procedure. The ritual included a demonstration of male physical prowess and was taken as a challenge of their manhood by the men who went into the enclosure. Everyone else watched from the stands.

Although Vicky started off in the stands as a spectator, she wasn't able to stay there, especially as the process could get quite rough on the frightened horses and the foals were in physical danger until they could be located and separated out. She had heard that there was controversy surrounding continuing to hold this very popular festival, and she could clearly see why there was. It was seeing a man having trouble pulling a foal out of a swarm of milling frightened horses and hearing the foal's plaintive whiney that brought Vickie out of her seat and down into the enclosure.

"Here, the poor dear is frightened to death," she cried out as she waded into the teeming mass, quickly told the man she knew how to work horses, put her arms around the foal's neck, and whispered calming sounds into its ear. The foal stopped trembling and she and the man were able to pull it to safety. As she reached the edge of the enclosure, another man brushed up against her, put a hand out to prevent her from being butted by a reeling horse, and gave her a broad smile. It was Uxio Silva, who was in the enclosure with the other men, working with the horses as one of the adoitadores.

Is there nothing he doesn't do, she wondered.

She smiled wanly back at him as she helped guide the foal to the other pen. When she'd done so, she turned and looked back into the main enclosure and saw that Uxio was having difficulty now trapping and containing a particularly large and heavily muscled wild horse, a white stallion, which undoubtedly would be the pride of the festival the next year after it had been tamed—if it could be tamed. The three men trying to wrestle it into submission so the cutting ritual could be performed on it had their hands full. Uxio looked particularly vulnerable to being pulled underneath the horse and to feel the strike of it hooves.

Vicky waded into the enclosure once again and made her way to that horse.

"No, you shouldn't be in here. It's too dangerous. Go back," Uxio cried out to her. Although not impeccable, his English was easily understandable. She would have been helpless trying to figure out what he was saying if he only spoke Spanish.

"Here, let me help," she stubbornly cried out. "The horse is just terrified. Let me help you quiet him down. I have a way with horses. I rescue ones as frightened as this."

And she did have a way with the white stallion. She threw her arm around its neck, just as she had done with the foal, and whispered to it and stroked it. Although it took time, the wildness that was in the beast's eyes toned down and it stopped trembling and stood there, in the embrace of Uxio, another man, and Vicky, as the fourth man cut its mane and tail, and inserted the tag in its ear.

When they were done, they let the horse go. It snorted and tossed its head up and down and was gone. The two nameless men who had worked on the horse with Vicky and Uxio, harnessed it and pulled it out of the ring to go to the holding corral for those horses that had gone through the ritual.

"He's magnificent," Vicky exclaimed as the horse was led away.

"You're the one who is magnificent," Uxio said, putting his hand on her arm. "But now, women aren't permitted in the enclosure. It's too dangerous, and it isn't permitted at the festival. Let me take to you the side before we have more than the wild horses to worry about."

He did so, and Vicky docilely went with him. Once they were out of the enclosure, they stood there, their eyes locked in some sort of unspoken understanding of each other. Vicky thought then that he would try to kiss her, and she didn't struggle long with the thought of whether she would let him do it. But someone called his name from within the enclosure, and he turned and was lost inside the teeming mass of horses still to be processed.

Suddenly Vicky was very tired, and as interesting as the rituals of this festival were, they made her a bit uneasy. The horses were frightened, if only for a while, not knowing that some of them would go to an easier life than being at the mercy of the elements, that those with a medical issue would be sent for treatment, and that those that were released back to the wild would have less competition for another year for food and natural shelter.

When she went back to her friends in the stands, she found them saying that they'd seen enough—even Denise's new boyfriend, Anton, agreed with that. They were all ready to climb into their rented car, go back to the Torre do Rio Hotel in Caldas de Reis, and hit the swimming pool.

As they were leaving, Vicky looked around for another sighting of Uxio Silva, but he was nowhere to be seen.

* * * *

The festival was over. The four, who were now five, with the addition of Anton Vasquez plastered to Denise's side, were relaxing from their A Rapa das Bestas festival adventure around a table in the ruins by the pool at the Torre do Rio Hotel. All were weary—Vicky, Peggy, and Sabela most likely weary from a different form of exercise than Denise and Anton were—and content with sitting, drinking wine, admiring the atmospherics around them, and listening to the guitar music and the mellow singing. Once again, the entertainer was Uxio Silva, seemingly bottomless in energy since he had been more active in the festival rituals than any of the rest of them had been.

Once again Uxio seemed to be singing and playing directly for Vicky, and now Vicky was openly acknowledging the attention.

"Two more days to take in the rest of Galicia and then back on the plane to Virginia," Peggy said, with a deep sigh. "We should have listened to Sabela, I guess, and booked for a longer stay. There's so much to see here in Galicia. It's all so fascinating."

"I think I will stay a bit longer," Vicky announced to her companions out of the blue. I've called Alec and he claims to be doing well and would be just as happy if I extended my vacation here.

"What do you . . . oh," Sabela started to say, but when Denise nudged her with an elbow and tilted her head toward where Uxio Silva was sitting, Sabela snapped her jaw shut.

"Although I guess I might have trouble changing my airplane reservation," Vicky continued.

Denise jumped on that. "We could go to the travel agency and see if the name can be switched on your reservation. I can pay you for your seat and then you can just book for later."

"What do you need with another . . . oh." It was Peggy's turn to have her question stifled by a nudge of the elbow from Sabela and a titling of Sabela's head toward Anton.

The music had stopped and Uxio was being replaced by another entertainer. He was putting his equipment together, ready to leave, but he stopped and looked over to their table. As the other entertainer, a woman, started to play and sing an ancient Galician ballad in a mournful voice, Uxio came over to the table and reached a hand out to Vicky.

"Gustaríache bailar comigo, fermosa?" he said, smiling at Vicky.

"He's asking whether you—" Sabela started to explain.

"I know what he's asking," Vicky said. "I would be delighted," she spoke to Uxio with a smile of her own as she rose, he guided her to the terrace by the pool, and he swept her up into a close dance embrace. It wouldn't have mattered what music was being performed.

POETRY

The Rampant Calabaza

By Liza Grantham

I thought I'd grow some vegetables outside my rural *casa*:
Potatoes, carrots, lettuce, and perhaps a *calabaza*.
I dug the garden in the spring and planted a *semilla*
I weeded carefully round it and I watered it each *día*.
A few weeks passed, and then I saw some leaves *aparecen*
My marrow plant was growing well. I shouted '*muy bien!*'
When Summer came I felt such pride, my plant was *buen crecido*,
Under its leaves the other veg had *desaparecido!*
Then very soon the marrows came, the size of my small *dedo*,
Then later, bigger than my leg, oh dear, *tenía miedo!*
The marrows flourished, for it seems they loved the rain and *sol*,
And soon the plant was very nearly big as an *arból*
Eventually, it did engulf the whole of my small *huerto*,
Potatoes, carrots, lettuce in its shadow now were *muerto*.
And now I've marrows in the lounge, the bedrooms and the *baño*;
Enough to feed the village for the whole of the next *año!*
I only wanted vegetables outside my rural *casa*
But my life's been taken over by the rampant *calabaza!*

The Four Elements for the Heaven

By Adrián Casanova Chiclana

I was blind like a Golem.
A day,
I discovered this paradise,
then begin to write this poem.
In this Mesopotamian land,
My soul feels,
the soft breeze,
the river Sil kiss.
I loved the sound
that was made by
the coal kitchen,
when the fire crackled.
Together, light the fire.
Our faces the fire reflects,
like smoked mirrors.
Now, the past shows it,
We speak about our world,
with heroic red wine,
without mobile phones.
How to get here? Follow the Winter route through
      sky lighthouses.

Our Peaceful Village

By Liza Grantham

At midnight
The breeze stirs the leaves on the chestnut tree,
Springs trickle,
Somewhere a mouse scurries along a beam
And our peaceful village sleeps.

At daybreak
A rooster heralds the arrival of a new day,
Birds twitter,
Somewhere an owl hoots from the oak wood
And our peaceful village yawns awake.

At breakfast
A car horn announces the delivery of mail,
Voices murmur,
Somewhere a gate creaks on rusty hinges
And our peaceful village shuffles to life.

All morning
A farmer bellows orders to the cattle,
Bells jingle,
Somewhere a dog barks a heedless warning
And our peaceful village rallies to its daily tasks.

All afternoon
A tractor clatters and rumbles with its load,
Chainsaws rattle,
Somewhere a concrete mixer churns its heaving belly
And our peaceful village bravely toils.

At sunset
Tired footsteps plod behind a clanking barrow,
Hooves stumble,
Somewhere a barn door groans shut wearily
And our peaceful village heaves a tired sigh.

At nightfall
A cat purrs lazily beside a glowing wood stove,
Logs crackle,
Somewhere a cork pops in reward for the day's labours
And our peaceful village rests at last.

At midnight
The breeze stirs the leaves on the chestnut tree,
Springs trickle,
Somewhere the same mouse scurries along a beam
And our peaceful village sleeps again.

My Dog Chased a Fox

By Liza Grantham

My dog chased a fox,
Heart beating, bounding through bracken,
Into the forest;
And I listened as the cracking of twigs and the rustling of leaves
Drifted further and further away.

My dog chased a deer,
Breath panting, pounding through pasture,
Into the forest;
And I listened as the cracking of twigs and the rustling of leaves
Drifted further and further away.

My dog chased a hawk,
Eyes shining, shifting through shadows,
Into the forest,
And I listened as the cracking of twigs and the rustling of leaves
Drifted further and further away.

My dog chased a boar,
Feet thumping, thundering through thicket,
Into the forest,
And I listened as the cracking of twigs and the rustling of leaves .
. .
The rustling of leaves . . .
The rustling . . .
Drifted nearer and nearer to me.

A boar chased my dog,
Bulk heaving, hurtling through hedgerow,
Out of the forest . . .
And I SCREAMED!!

A Drop

by J. P. Vincent

A drop falls
light reflecting
windows green.
Splashes on leaf
bounces to land and
darkening parched earth,
absorbed by brown minerals.
Others joining, collecting, flowing
these pearls of shimmer reflecting.
Trickling, dashing, leaping following
gradients,
joining others. Excited,
splattering, tumbling,
babbling, altering form.
Rills, rivulets, becks, rindles'
amassing shape,
fluid curving round obstacles moving
earth,
multiplying gaining depth in their headlong race.
Changing colour, green reflections to brown
collections,
slowing, twisting, widening past villages, towns and cities.
Their path obstructed, dammed by concrete, never
stopping.
Sometimes choked with effluent this pure tear absorbing
filth.
Widening to home fish and fowl, flattening out a sigh
meanders.
The journey's end to join with oceans blue, a single drop
magnified,
multiplied, its depth unfathomable, its width vast, its power
unchallenged.

Molten Tempest

by J. P. Vincent

Heat oppressive builds and grows
Climate change alters jet stream course
Man's abuse and theft now shows.

In readiness all objects are stowed.
A phenomenon from Sahara source
Heat oppressive builds and grows.

Veiled darkening sky wildly glows
Sand plucked in upward force
Man's abuse and theft now shows.

Winds whip dust, bar pressure lows
Fires finger through treetops course
Heat oppressive builds and grows.

Smoke curls, pall, obscure follows
Without relief no rain to endorse
Heat oppressive builds and grows
Man's abuse and theft now shows.

The Barn

By Liza Grantham

My Grandad built this barn himself,
With Uncle Juan and Dad,
Way back in nineteen twenty-seven,
When I was just a lad.

They built two walls to South and West
Of stones sealed up with mud,
The other walls to North and East
Of rough hewn chestnut wood.

I watched them toiling day by day
All heaving rocks and boulders,
Then up the ladder, rung by rung,
Huge stones across their shoulders.

Next came the roof: handcrafted tiles
Of clay dug from the land
Laid one by one, held fast with stones
On beams they'd sawn by hand.

The doors were hung on hinges forged
From iron by Uncle Juan,
Dad swung them closed, a perfect fit
Then told me, "Go fetch Gran!"

The barn complete we all stood back,
And gazed in admiration,
"I feel so proud," Gran beamed at us:
"Let's have a celebration!"
On Sunday she laid out a spread

On trestles where we'd dine
Chorizos, cheeses, ham and bread
And jugs of homemade wine.

So, after mass the throng arrived:
Our family, friends, and neighbours
Who raised their glasses to "the barn,
These men and all their labours!"

Then Uncle Juan struck up the pipes,
Muiñeras loudly ringing,
Our barn swelled with the happy sound
Of laughter, dancing, singing.

My grandad took me to one side,
"Manolo, wait and see:
This barn will last a hundred years,
'Til you're as old as me!"

Girl Talk

By Liza Grantham

The girls were gathered, waiting
For the stragglers to arrive,
Dolores sighed, "What's keeping them?
We've all been up since five!"

"You know what Clara's like," smiled Luz,
"She'll wait for poor Belén—
She's limping something terrible,
That dodgy knee again."

"I wonder where we're lunching?"
Angelina mused to Em.
"I'm guessing same as yesterday,
I s'pose it's up to *them*."

"I liked the other place we tried,
The one just up the hill,
The food just seemed so fresh compared
To that place by the mill."

"Oh no, they've brought that dog again,
I hate the wretched cur.
It bit Luz on the leg last week,
It always goes for her."

"It went for me as well," scowled Em.
"I didn't half see red!
I made sure they weren't looking
And I kicked its bloomin' head!"

"I think I'm pregnant!" Luz announced.
Belén smirked, "You get dafter!"
"No bull!" said Luz. "Precisely, dear!"
The others roared with laughter!

The lunch, al fresco, lasted hours—
They felt no need to hurry:
They nibbled, gossiped, ate some more,
And no-one seemed to worry.

Dolores sighed as they strolled home.
"I've had a lovely day!
But I'll be glad when milking's done,
Can't wait to hit the hay!"

About the Authors

Adrián Casanova Chiclana

Adrián Casanova Chiclana, Galician born, says he enjoys writing because he considers it a natural and silent means of communication among people who are far apart. Writing is a powerful tool, which can stir up intense feelings and emotions. He usually writes in the Galician language because he believes it is a breath of fresh air, reminiscent of the scent of damp earth after the first drops of rain. He has previously taken part in several competitions in this language, obtaining second place in the Xuventude Crea (2016), a short story competition organized by the Xunta de Galicia and being short-listed in the competition O Lugar Onde Vivo, Relatos polo Territorio (2014), organized by ADEGA Publishing and the Diputation of Lugo. He describes himself as an inquisitive person who has many interests and an entropy lover. For this reason, he belongs to a cultural association called Náufragos do Paradiso, which aims to turn the Ribeira Sacra into a cultural paradise besides being a place of natural beauty, of extensive Romanesque heritage and the cradle of the famous Ribeira Sacra wines. #P.S.:Love the Planet.

Bronwyn Cole

Bronwyn Cole was born and raised in New Zealand and spent all of her life there until the call of the Camino belatedly pulled her to Europe for her first big OE (overseas experience) in 2015. She has trained variously as a medical laboratory technician and an anthroposophical art therapist but found her way into working in her current job, as the factory coordinator for the New Zealand branch of Weleda, where she has been for more than seventeen years. She has one adult daughter, Celeste, who keeps her very busy with her renovating projects. Bronwyn lives in Otane, a small, semirural village in Central Hawke's Bay, with her Spanish partner, Fernando, two dogs, two cats, a collection of chickens, and too many fantail pigeons to count. Her favourite way to relax is pottering in her organic vegetable garden and hanging out with the birds, disappearing into a good book, or heading off to the local café for a coffee with Fernando.

Fiona Cowan

Fiona Cowan is from Orkney and has spent most of her life working there as an occuptional therapist. When their two sons set off for university, she and husband, Les Cowan, author of the David Hidalgo crime series, set off as grown-up gappers studying in New Zealand, London, and Madrid. Reaching Galicia in 2013, they teach English, collaborate with a small evangelical church in Ribadeo, and sail the Rias on sunny days. On wetter days she meets with local women to do patchwork or to teach baking classes. She is only motivated to write for competitions and prefers to write in Orcadian, usually poetry. She enjoys the prizes more than seeing her work published or broadcast. She plans to return to the UK in 2018, stop blogging, and take more exercise!

Robin Hillard

Australian Author, Robin Hillard, grew up in Western Australia goldfields and has lived in provincial cities and towns of various sizes during a career spent teaching in Australia, England, and Canada. She has now settled, with her husband, in Toowoomba, which is known as the garden city of Queensland. It is well served with antique shops and provides inspiration for her mystery stories and puzzles. Toowoomba also provides a site for the Australian town of Ridgeway, which features in her mystery novel, *Ridgeway Murder*. Robin also writes science fiction and reviews poetry for *Polestar Magazine*.

Andrea Jones

Andrea Jones was born in the UK but grew up in Galicia. She left the UK at the age of seven with her mother and stepfather and, after traveling throughout Europe and other parts of Spain, they settled in a small village close to the town of Monforte de Lemos. Mother of four, she has lived for different periods in Burgos and other parts of Galicia, including a short time in Muxía on the famous Death Coast. Finally having returned to Monforte de Lemos, she currently works as a teacher of both English and Spanish. She enjoys writing in her spare time.

Noelia Roca Jones

Noelia Roca Jones was born to an English mother and Galician father in a small town in the south of the Galician province of Lugo. She grew up listening to the fascinating legends of the darkest Galician folklore. She is a qualified carer and has worked looking after elderly people both privately and in various nursing homes. However, after a placement in a school for children with special needs, she decided to retrain as a nursery teacher. She is currently doing a two-year college course. She thought this competition was an excellent opportunity to tell other people one of Galicia's most famous legends and hopes to continue writing in the future.

J. P. Vincent

J. P. Vincent is the penname of Jacqueline Suffolk. A bubbly British blonde, Jacqueline now lives in Galicia, with her sainted partner, John. They share life with a Galician cat called Freddie who was found living, with his mum, under their roof. They spend their time renovating their old stone house, rebuilding barns, and also 200 meters of dry stone walling, which to date they've completed about a tenth of. They also have half a mountain to do something with when they run out of other things to do.

Jacqueline loves to travel. She and John spent many years touring Europe in their motorhome, La Gorda, and she loves to write about travelling. Her bus route No.83 article is in the latest edition of the Bradt Travel Guide "Bus Pass Britain." She is also a consultant for Motorhome Monthly Magazine (MMM) where her remit is to answer queries regarding motorhome travel in northern Spain and Portugal.

Olivia Stowe

Olivia is a published author under different names and in other dimensions of fiction and non-fiction and lives quietly in a university town with an indulgent spouse.

She is the author of the best selling Charlotte Diamond Mystery Series.

You can find Olivia at CyberworldPublishing.com.

The Good Life in Galicia (2016)

In e-book and paperback from all online bookstores.

The
Good Life
in Galicia

An Anthology

Edited by S. Bush